FOOD FOR OUR JOURNEY

HOMILIES VOLUME I:
THE DESERT EXPERIENCE

MOST REV. DR. CHARLES JASON GORDON

Sophronismos Press
Louisville, Kentucky, USA

First Printing: February 2021

ISBN: 978-1-7335457-5-4

ADDRESS:
27 Maraval Rd
Maraval
Trinidad and Tobago
Caribbean

Email: abcjg@catholictt.org

**Other books by Archbishop Gordon may be found on
Amazon.com**

Encounters of Grace: A Pilgrim's Musing Along
The Camino de Santiago

Meditations in the Upper Room

Teach Us to Pray

Birthing the Word of God:
A Little Book on Christian Preaching

TABLE OF CONTENTS

ACKNOWLEDGEMENTS

I wish to thank the many people who gave me feedback during this extraordinary year. Your encouragement assisted me greatly in keeping on track with preparation and delivery to television every day. It was both a work of love and a grace. Special thanks here to Derek Hudson, Candice Clarke-Salloum and Carla Mendez who gave real-time feedback during those early days, assisting me to better reach people and ensure the Mass was a focal point in the life of many people by creating a sense of community and asking people to respond to specific needs.

Thanks to Karen Ann Hadad Ready, Peggy Guiseppi, Natalie Jacob, Cheryl Kam, Donna-Kay Kissoon, Natasha Margaret Lake, the transcription team, who moved the text from oral to written, laying the first foundation for this book.

To Sr. Deborah De Rosia, who prayerfully mulled over the work three times, strengthening the language and bringing the individual homilies together into a book. To Laura Ann Phillips, for your diligence in proofreading the text, preparing it for publication.

Fr. Ronald Knott, thanks for the support through the Second Wind Guild that has made the publishing of this book possible. Thanks, also, to Tim Schoenbachler who did the technical work and graphic design to bring the manuscript to a book and publication.

This ministry and the compilation of the homilies would not have been possible without the generosity and technical skill of Trinity Television and their crew, who came to my chapel at 6:00 a.m. every morning to prepare for filming.

They were the first receivers of the Mass and the first to give feedback, which led to continuous improvement. Thanks, also, to the choirs and those who planned them every day. This, too, was a work of love which contributed to God's feeding that we all benefitted from.

Most of all, glory be to God, whose grace working in us can do infinitely more than we can ask or imagine (cf. Eph. 3:20).

INTRODUCTION

On March 13, 2020, I awoke and had the haunting feeling that I was terribly late for the party. The COVID-19 party! I had Mass at 6:30 a.m. in the chapel and, right after, spoke to Derek Hudson and arranged for him and two other leaders of the energy sector to meet with key members of my staff, other professionals and doctors. At 1:00 p.m., sharp, we began the meeting: Fr. Martin Sirju, the vicar general; Sharon Mangroo, the CEO of our Education Board; Deacons Roy and Lennox, who lead the Chancery and the Departments; Raymond Syms of CAMSEL – our communications arm; Dr. Rolph Balgobin, a strategic thinker, who kept niggling me on the escalation of the virus; Dr. Patrick Campbell, a local infectious disease specialist and Dr. John McNeil, an infectious disease specialist in Maryland, who happens to be my brother-in-law.

Dr. McNeil was already treating cases of COVID-19 and was horrified by the resistance of the virus to anything they tried. He had already lost many patients and it was clear that the science, at that stage, was powerless once people reached to ventilators. Dr. Patrick introduced us to the R0 factor: COVID-19 was more infectious than the common cold. Each person who contracted it would likely spread it to three people. This meant exponential spread.

The energy sector is at the cutting edge with Health, Safety and Environment (HSE); it is core to their business. Eugene Okpere of Shell, Vince Pereira of BHP with Derek Hudson, former Vice-President at Shell, all engaged the conversation with the growing realisation of the severity of the situation. After an hour, we called the meeting to a close with a clear sense of direction. The energy CEOs went back to their offices to send their people home to work remotely. We were closing schools and churches with immediate effect.

By 2:30, we contacted the Minister of Education and the Minister of National Security who, themselves, were in high-level conversations about COVID-19. They had come to the same conclusion: schools and churches needed to close as they were, potentially, super-spreaders. By 2:45, we had a statement written and Sharon went back to CEBM (Catholic Education Board of Management) to send a memo to all principals and staff of Catholic schools that we were closing schools until further notice. We had done the internal debate; we understood the consequences on both sides of the argument and we were resolved to do the right thing.

Just after 3:00, we had finished polishing the release to close the parishes. As we were about to send it, Deacon Lennox said, "You better hold it." "Why?" we all asked. Pope Francis had just released a statement that we believed went completely against our deliberation and intended actions. A Zenit report claimed the Pope said, "Drastic measures are not always good." Therefore, he prayed the Holy Spirit would "grant pastoral discernment to pastors so that they might perceive measures that might not leave the holy, faithful people of God alone, and so that people of God might feel accompanied by their pastors." (*Zenit*. March 13, 2020.) This was a game-changer! In the heat of the moment, we paused.

Everything in the science told me to close the churches and the schools; the Holy Father was taking us in a different direction. A pastoral direction that challenged my assumptions and, it seemed, the decision we made and were about to implement. We debated back and forth till about 5:00 p.m. Then, with a very heavy heart, issued the decree to close the schools and issued a statement to keep the churches very safe and asked people who had symptoms to stay at home.

That night, in a conversation with a person asking why I was not closing the churches I said, "You ever made a decision and had your leader throw you a curve ball in mid-action? As a priest, I took a vow of obedience to my bishop. As a bishop, I live a vow of obedience to the Pope. I was confronted with two values: obedience, and keeping my people safe in a pandemic. They seemed to conflict. I erred on the side of obedience."

I was teaching those in formation for the diaconate on Saturday morning. We shifted to online sessions and began class at 9:00. Because of the preparation necessary, I asked the Vicar General, Fr. Martin, to dig deeper into what the Pope said and to find a solution. At about 10:45 a.m., while on a break, Fr. Martin and I spoke. He and I tossed the matter back and forth, seeing both sides of the conundrum. Then, while I was teaching, they did the research on the statement of the Pope. Now, in the cool of the day, it was clearer: he was speaking of the Church as a shelter for the poor and refuge for the needy. He did not promote keeping the churches open for Masses!

When the class was over, Fr. Martin and I spoke. He had two decrees prepared: one to keep the churches open and the second to close them. I have worked my whole life to bring people to church. The decision to close the churches, to tell people not to go to church, was gut-wrenching. I agonised about that decision more than any decision I have made in my time as a bishop. By 2:00 p.m. on Saturday, we closed the churches indefinitely and sent the word out to all priests and on the media to the people. I also sent it to a few of the other Christian leaders. The deed had been done. It was a very long twenty-five hours. Science and obedience were served well.

On Saturday afternoon, I arranged with Trinity Television that I would do the Sunday Mass for television. That Sunday morning, driving to the chapel to say Mass, my radio was on. There was a Pentecostal preacher on the radio saying, "Those leaders hold high office, but, they are not disciples in obedience to Christ. If they were disciples, they would know that no pandemic could stop the work of God." Here, again, faith and science were in conversation, and science was given short shrift. The preacher paraded on the likes of me – a Christian Church leader who did not believe that Christ was more powerful than COVID. In the US, several pastors took this position, and we know several died from COVID, also killing some of their congregation. Between faith and science, there is wisdom and prudence. God has asked us to use all of who we are to lead His people to salvation.

On the Saturday afternoon, I also arranged that Trinity would send a crew every day to record and televise the daily Mass from my chapel. It was just instinct that, if the churches were closed, we needed to reach the people where they were. Pastorally, it was the most fruitful decision I made as a bishop. Every day, Monday to Friday, Trinity sent two persons to record the Mass. On Sundays, I went to their chapel to do the Sunday Mass. Whereas one camera served for Monday to Friday, Sunday had to be special, with three cameras.

That first Sunday, March 15, I was apprehensive. We planned the Mass with one reader, a choir of two, a deacon and myself. This was to comply with the stipulated five-person maximum regulation. Saying Mass to an empty church seemed daunting. I asked the reader to sit in front of the camera, so that I would have someone to watch and, hopefully, feedback while I was celebrating and preaching. It was painful at first! Then, after a few Masses, I imagined a crowd of people inside of the camera. I began looking straight at the camera and preaching. There was grace in abundance. There was anointing. God was feeding His people through the word. The Word was becoming flesh and He made His dwelling amongst us.

After Mass, that first Sunday, we sat and debriefed. Then, some of the camera crew began playing with the word COVID. Very quickly, Christ Our Victory In the Desert popped out. That was the theme for the first part of the Journey – the desert. It was where the readings took us during Lent. It was as if God had arranged the timing, and God was in charge. We were all nurtured by the richness of this grace.

During the time of the COVID lockdown, I spent more and more time preparing the daily homily. I soon realised that each homily needed to be like a Sunday homily – fully fleshed out, an exposition on the scripture where people are invited to encounter the living God. So many people said it was a grace for them. The truth is, it was an incredible grace for me! Mulling over the Word of God every day, reading the best commentaries and searching for The Word that God wanted to speak to His people became for me a grace that was rich and delightful. I am very happy to share with you this work, the fruit of that period of COVID grace. Through this time, we made a journey together – bishop and people. This gave rise to the name, "Food for the Journey".

In our Catholic Tradition, "Food for Our Journey" has many connections. It evokes what God did for the people during the Exodus (Ex. 16) – He gave them manna to eat every day in the desert. This daily feeding was a matter of life and death for the people of the Exodus. For many people plunged into the desert of the COVID-19 pandemic, the daily bread of the word was a gift from God that sustained us on our journey. Every day, I was fed by the word. Every day, I fed the people. For Bishop and people it was, indeed, "Food for Our Journey". There is a second connection – *Viaticum*. This is Latin for "food for the journey". It refers to the Eucharist that is given to the sick person in the *Sacrament of the Anointing of the Sick*. It is given to assist them in making their journey to God. This, too, we all experienced. Every day, we were fed. Every day, we made our journey to God.

I need to say a word about the language in this book. For me, the homily is a spoken art. It is conceived in prayer and research, and born in the delivery. In Trinidad, our everyday speech is a Creolised English. The Nobel laureates Derek Walcott and Sir V.S Naipaul would argue it is not a bastardised form of English but, rather, a language in its own right, with its own internal rules and syntax. Dr. Lise Winer of the Faculty of Education, McGill University, edited and published "*Dictionary of the English/Creole of Trinidad and Tobago*", 2009. This is a 1,039-page work that defines words

14

that are unique to Trinidad and Tobago. This scholarly work has demonstrated that the English Creole of Trinidad and Tobago can stand scholarly scrutiny for its coherence and consistency in definition, rhythm and syntax.

I preach in Trinidadian Creole. This is by deliberate choice. In the Acts of the Apostles at Pentecost, it says: "How is it that all of us hears them in his own native language?" (Acts 2:8). In England, a preacher in Oxford speaks very differently from a preacher in the East End of London. Both speak to their hearers in their unique idiom.

In translating the homily to written form, we made the editorial decision to keep the Trinidad Creole of the original homilies, rather than attempt to translate it into standard Oxford English. Most English speakers will be able to follow the text with little challenge. Caribbean People will find, in the text, a resonance that we do not always experience. Do not let the language distract you. It is standard Trinidadian Creole English.

The book has a simple structure; there is an appetiser: the first Sunday of Lent. This gives the foundation for the plunge into the desert of COVID. Then, we read each week of Lent culminating in Holy Week and Easter Vigil Mass. There is an addendum: the Chrism Mass, which was celebrated on November 9 this year. This Mass is an integral part of the Holy Week celebrations and was included for that reason.

It is my prayer that, by reading this text, you will relive the grace we experienced during those days. I pray that this is an invitation to faith and to live your faith more deeply.

January 10, 2021.
The Feast of the Baptism of Our Lord.

APPETISER -
FIRST SUNDAY OF LENT

Temptation in the Desert

Sunday March 01, 2020.
First Sunday of Lent.

First Reading: Gen. 2: 7–9; 3:1–7
Responsorial Psalm: Psalm 50
Second Reading: Rom. 5:12–19
Gospel: Matt. 4:1–11
HOMILY: Archbishop Jason Gordon

Aren't you all excited? It is the First Sunday of Lent; this is the most exciting time in the Church! We get the opportunity for prayer, for fasting and for almsgiving! Aren't you all just excited? This is as great as it gets; you don't get it better than this.

Our readings today put in sharp context what it is we're working with here. In Lent, the first reading and the gospel reading connect and, what we have is a first reading that speaks about the big moments of salvation. So, in this case, we have the story of the Fall and the reason why we need to do prayer, fasting and almsgiving. Our gospel reading gives us the root cause of all of the challenges that we are facing and Jesus taking that on to Himself. So, let's look at these readings again and see how this works.

Many people will think, "If He was really God, could He really be tempted?" But, remember, in our Creed we say He is true God, true Man. He is like us in every single way, except for sin. And so, yes, He can be tempted; He was tempted and the temptations were real. So, He is out in the desert for forty days and that already should give us all kinds of connections, because we know the people wandered in the desert for forty years. Forty is this wonderful, biblical number that keeps appearing. He is out there and the scriptures say, "…He was hungry. " Worse than that, it says: *"... the Spirit led Him out into the desert for forty days and forty nights to be tempted by the devil"*. Wow! You got that one? Just like the Spirit leads us into these forty days of Lent, to be tempted by the devil.

Yes, the whole purpose of Lent is to up our game and to face the temptations. You see, by the end of Lent, you know just how much you need a Saviour. Now, you think you are just okay and all is well but, by the end of Lent, if you really do the thing well, you will know exactly how much you need a Saviour. And, by the end of Lent, you will know His name, too, because you will be calling it day in and day out! His name is Jesus Christ.

Our readings pose something for us that is really powerful. Jesus faces these three temptations. One: to turn stone into bread and, remember, He is very hungry. The second is to jump and, *"As You jump,"* He is being told, *"God will support You and everybody is going to see that You are the real deal because You could fly! And, You are going to come down with a real soft landing and everybody is just going to be totally amazed and we are going to know that You are the real deal!"* And, the third one is to bow, to bow before Satan and, if He does that, He will be given all the kingdoms of the world. That means all the kings – which means all the peoples of the world – will be handed to Him. Remember,

18

Jesus' mission is to bring all humanity back to God. His mission is to bring all humanity back to God! And, Satan is saying, *"You could do that without any cross. You could do it without the cross, just bow. Give a little knee, come on! Just bow!"* Here we have, in these temptations, the very heart, source and substance of the challenge that humanity faces.

In our first reading from Genesis, we hear the way that the human fell and, you know, it had to do with food! Yes, like the first temptation, it had to do with food. There was a tree, it was the Tree of Knowledge; it looked good, they were tempted and they yielded to the temptation. There are three reasons why they yielded to the temptation that our reading teaches us: because the fruit looked good, it was pleasing to the eye and it was desirable for the knowledge it would give. So, they had three reasons and three temptations; Jesus has three temptations. Anybody connecting the dots?

If you look at the First Letter of John, Chapter 2, John expounds on this; he talks about the lust of the flesh, the lust of the eye and the pride of life. A Jew in the first century would have understood these three that are called, in the tradition, concupiscence. Concupiscence refers to these disordered desires that we have, disordered desires that have come from the Genesis story, because it is in the Genesis story that the disordered desires led to the rebellion against God, to the Fall and to the mayhem that we have lived ever since the Fall. Do you ever ask yourself why Adam and Eve were so stupid? It would have been so nice: all of us in paradise, everybody happy, no murder, no mayhem, no foolishness, no nothing – everybody living so nice with everybody else! But, concupiscence entered into the human and continued to enter into the human. Jesus goes into the desert and faces concupiscence – the three-fold temptation – and, rather than give into concupiscence like Adam and Eve did, like all of humanity does, Jesus resists.

The first of the three temptations is lust of the flesh: *"Turn the stone into bread because You are hungry. Use Your power, man!"* We know that Jesus had no problem with bread because He fed the 5,000. And, another time, He fed 4,000 with bread. The problem is not in Him doing stuff with bread, the problem is the temptation to use His power for Himself which is, really, giving into the lust for food, to gluttony, giving into a disordered desire. And, the lust of the flesh – I do not think we have to look far in Trinidad to understand what that means. If you need me to break this down for you, just go back to some time earlier last week and just look at any television or pictures you could find; you will understand what I am talking about.

The lust of the eye is the desire for things and, look at the temptation, that: "I will give You all the kingdoms of the world." *All! That is lust of the eye because, "I will give You all that the world has: money, power – I will give You all that You can have!"* That is, really, at the root of the advertising agency today. They promote lust of the eye in a way that is totally disordered because, unless you buy "this" product, you know you cannot find salvation – you know that! Because this is the one product that will give you the salvation you need by changing your hair or by smoothing your face or whatever the product is doing; they promote the lust of the eye. We live in a civilisation where we have actually turned concupiscence into a virtue. That is the heart of what is wrong in our society today.

You know, if anyone at all – archbishop, anybody – challenges the disordered desires and the lust and the depravity on Carnival Monday and Tuesday, there are many, many people who will get up publicly to defend the depravity that happens on the streets of Port of Spain! It has become a culture. And, not only has it become a culture, we can no longer see right from wrong; we cannot distinguish that there is appropriate behaviour on Monday and Tuesday, and there is inappropriate behaviour on Monday and Tuesday. And, because we cannot make that distinction, because wider society is really pushing hard at "free-license" – at people having a right to do whatever they want to do, wherever they want to do it – because that is the dominant force of our society, we have fallen into lust of the flesh. We have made it a culture and we have canonised it as if it were actually a virtue. That is undoing us as a civilisation – it is undoing us!

A lot of the mayhem in our society started with lust of the flesh; that is where it starts. It starts with a kind of creeping value system where lust becomes so canonised and so ordinary and, in fact, so desirable by the society that we continue with a way of believing that we can go for any material gain that we want. Get rich or die trying! We go for all kinds of things, pleasures that are absolutely disordered, creating communities where the children are not being mentored and parented in a way that allows them to grow up to be decent human beings and great citizens of the country. So, this business of concupiscence is at the very root of what is wrong in Trinidad and Tobago today, and we have taken it and put it on steroids. And, until we are willing, as a society, to say that disordered lust is wrong and let us, as a nation, do something about it, let us, as individuals, do something about it

– until we are willing to say to our children: "You know, that one is just a little too skimpy"; unless the parents are willing to say that to their children and grandchildren – we are promoting the lust of the flesh, the lust of the eye as if it were a great value. We are not saying anything, and the children are getting the signal from us that this is okay.

Pride of life: where He is asked to go to the parapet of the temple and jump because, *"Then, everybody will see."* And, there is nothing wrong with Him floating, you know, because He walked on water. But it is for everybody to see, and then, for everybody to big Him up because everybody sees. The reason why we engage in prayer, fasting and almsgiving is because prayer is the only antidote there is to pride. When you bow your heart to God, you also take a vaccination against pride. Fasting is the best antidote against lust of the flesh. Deprive yourself of food and of drink, or social media screens or the things you desire the most; depriving yourself of that is the best antidote to lust of the eye. Almsgiving covers a multitude of sins. Give what you have to those who do not have; it is the best antidote to concupiscence.

The three practices are not here because we like to have them. The three practices are here because we need them. Not only one or two or the other; the three practices together is what helps us to bring concupiscence to sharp focus and conversion of heart to what we actually need to become. In fasting, the tradition teaches two lines: one is abstinence, where we do without meat; the other is where we deprive ourselves of food. The tradition teaches two collations and one meal, and the two collations cannot add up to as much as a single meal would be – and you could go with much less than that. It is choosing to deprive yourself of food, of screen time, of something during this period of Lent. It could also be choosing to deprive yourself of a wicked tongue, or choosing to deprive yourself of nagging somebody, or choosing to deprive yourself of going negative on other people. It could be something in the attitudes that you choose to not partake in during this period of Lent, but prayer, fasting and abstinence come together as the best antidote to the experience of concupiscence.

We are all terrified of the coronavirus, but we not terrified of concupiscence! I want to tell you: the coronavirus might kill you, but concupiscence will send you to hell. We should be far more terrified of concupiscence than we are of catching any virus! We should be far more sensitive to concupiscence than we are of any virus that is flying around this place. Until the Christian becomes sensitive to concupiscence and understands its disordered desires and its ill effect in the soul, how it separates us from God, until we understand that, we will not be living as mature Christians. And, the whole point of Lent is to grow up spiritually.

So, let us get excited. Let us get real excited! Because we have an incredible opportunity in this Lent to grow up spiritually, to have eyes that actually see the truth of what God is putting before us and a heart that is converted to him. Amen.

*Lockdown of churches began on March 14th, 2020; consequently, there were no recorded homilies between the First and Third Sundays of Lent.

THIRD WEEK OF LENT

THE WOMAN AT THE WELL

Sunday March 15, 2020.
Third Sunday of Lent.

First Reading: Exodus 17: 3-7
Responsorial Psalm: Psalm 95: 1-2, 6-9
Second Reading: Romans 5: 1-2, 5-8
Gospel: John 4: 5-42
HOMILY: Archbishop Charles Jason Gordon

Our readings today are such amazing readings! The people wanted to stone Moses: *"How could you stop us from coming to Mass?"* Well, poor Moses, but God said, *"Take the leaders, go to the front of the community, and lead."* That is what we have to do in a time as challenging as this. When we started Lent, the word of that First Sunday of Lent was: *"Led by the Spirit, Jesus went into the desert for forty days to be tempted by the devil."* Do you remember that first gospel? Led by the Holy Spirit, Jesus went into the desert for forty days, where He ate nothing, to be tempted by the devil. That is really the context of where we are now. We can't forget that this is a Lenten time; we can't forget that, in this Lenten time, we are in a time of desert. I think it's important – as we are fasting from Eucharist – to understand that the desert is what Jesus, Himself, experienced in His forty days and, it is what the people experienced in their thirsting for God. My prayer is that these days of fast, where we will not be coming together as Church for Eucharist, will be a time where we would not allow that hunger to dissipate, but we would feel more acutely our hunger and our thirst for God. And, in feeling that hunger and thirst for God, we will seek God in every way that we can. That is the whole message of our gospel reading and, what a beautiful reading!

The reading has many, many layers. The first layer I would like to approach is the identity of Jesus. Who is this man Jesus Christ? Who is He? As you peel away the layers of the reading, the woman first saw Jesus as an open-minded Jew. *"What! You, a Jew, talking to me, a Samaritan woman?"* She saw Him as an open-minded Jew because Jews did not talk to Samaritans, far less to Samaritan women! Then, the next thing she says is: *"Wait, you think you are a greater man, a better man, than our ancestor Jacob, who drank from this well with all his family?"* Now, she moves from seeing Him as an open-minded Jew to someone who is greater than her ancestor Jacob, the patriarch of all of Israel. She has elevated Him.

Then she says, "I see, sir, you are a prophet." Now, she has advanced to His being a prophet, someone who is a voice of God. Ultimately, she comes to the realisation that He is the Christ, revealed by Jesus when He says, "I who am speaking to you, I am He." Jesus invokes the "I AM", which is the name by which God revealed Himself to Moses: "I AM Who AM". And, in that revelation, Jesus is now revealing to this woman His true identity, not just as the Messiah, but also, as God. The double reference in the statement helps the woman to see that this man, Jesus, is not just an open-minded Jew, not just "a greater man than our ancestor, Jacob," not just a prophet, but He is both the Messiah – for whom we have been waiting – and He is God. With that, she drops her jar and goes back to the village. Now, a water jar is a precious, precious thing; without water, you die. So, to leave behind her water jar and go back to the village is to experience something that is significantly different.

The second level of the text now: the Samaritans were a mixed-race people resulting from the intermarriage of Jews and Gentiles, and the Jews looked down on them. They practiced a funny kind of faith in which they believed in the God of Israel, but not as their only God because they had other gods. In this level of the text, what we see is really the greatest challenge to the Church today: how do we transmit faith from person to person, and how do we transmit faith from person to community? This is one of the best stories we have of it. As Jesus engages this woman and she comes to faith, she goes back into the village and she tells everybody about what this man says. They come back to Jesus and they say, *"We believed You because of her testimony, but we no longer believe because of her testimony alone; having encountered You ourselves we now believe because we have experienced You."* That is what transmission of faith is.

How many of you have given your faith to your children and, for many years, your children believed in Jesus because of what you taught them? But the ultimate transmission of the faith is when your child comes to say to you: "I believed in this man Jesus because of what you said, but now, having encountered Him myself, I no longer believe because of you, I believe because I have met Him myself." That is the piece in our catechetical formation that's not working as well as it should, because we are not giving the faith to the next generation where they come to the personal belief in Jesus themselves; not based on what you say, but on what Jesus, Himself, has done in their lives.

Everybody is talking about the coronavirus, because the coronavirus is one of the most infectious diseases that we have ever seen in the world. The common cold will infect 1.3 persons for every person who is infected. Coronavirus infects 2.2 people for every person who is infected. And, I believe, I believe that the Gospel of Jesus Christ is more infectious than coronavirus! I believe that! I believe that if every person who has taken the Gospel of Jesus Christ to their heart, brings that Gospel to 2.2 people and those bring it to 2.2 people, we would do better than the woman at the well, and she converted a whole village. Now, that is a very infectious spread of the Gospel of Jesus Christ! The virus is teaching us something: we have to be more active, so that more people come to know the Gospel of Jesus Christ and encounter that Gospel as a life-giving Gospel from which they can live their whole life and upon which they can put everything. And, if we do that, then the Gospel itself takes a new life and goes forward in a new way. That is only the second level.

On another level, the woman is talking about water. And, on this level, what we are hearing is a wonderful discourse where Jesus is playing with the woman and the woman is playing with Him, because they are at a well. She is saying: *"You know, sir, you come here telling me you could give me a drink but you have no bucket; how are you giving me a drink and you have no bucket?"* He responded, "If you knew who was asking and what it is that He was offering, you would be the one asking and I will give you living water." Jesus moves from the water in the well to Living Water and, in this interplay, Jesus is speaking about something that is so precious. At the very heart of the Christian life is what is called by the tradition, Christ-life. Christ-life is the life of grace that lives in us. As we develop and grow in faith, Christ-life grows and, as Christ-life grows, it pushes out ego, it pushes out temptation, it pushes out other things and takes the space at the centre of our life where Christ becomes square and centre of everything in our life. That is what the living water is: it is this life of grace that wells up inside of the person, nourishes the person and brings that person deeper into the intimacy with God. But, to explore that I have to go to the next level.

On this other level, the disciples were very perturbed when they saw Jesus talking to the woman at the well. They say to each other: *"What is He doing here talking to this woman?"* And, in that moment, the disciples are now ashamed, anxious for their Master sitting by a well, talking to the woman. You see, in the Old Testament, when you meet a man and a woman by a well, the next thing that happens is marriage. Jacob, when he came to that same well and he met his future wife, the next text in the Bible was the marriage of Jacob. When Moses walked through the desert and came to his father-in-law, Jethro, it was at the well he met his future wife. You see, in those days, if a single man was looking for an eligible wife a well was a really good place to go to meet them, because that is where they used to be. So, a man and a woman at a well is trouble, and the disciples understood this. They understood this was a little bit raunchy – *"There is something in there we can't quite cope with."* But the story in St. John takes this theme of the nuptial union that takes place at a well to a very different level. Because this woman, when Jesus confronts her and says, "Go and bring your husband," she responds: *"Sir, I don't know how to tell You this but, yes, I have had five husbands, but the one I am living with now is not really my husband"* – can you imagine the embarrassment in this?

You see, the Samaritan people had five different gods. They flirted with the God of Israel, but they also had five other gods. If you remember the prophet Hosea who compared the abandonment of God to idolatry, to prostitution, said, "You have forsaken Me for these gods that have no power." The covenant between God and His people is compared to marriage and, therefore, the breaking of marriage with idolatry is compared to adultery. That is what Jesus is introducing here. The woman who has these five husbands, five other gods, is breaking the covenant that they made with the God of the Jews. And that idolatry that she is living with these five other gods, not quite holding to the true God, Jesus is inviting her to leave, inviting her back to worship the one true God. Seeing Himself as the bridegroom, the woman now becomes the type of the bride, because she is part Jew, part Gentile, representing the whole Church. She is now the type of the Church that encompasses all the nations that He espouses here in this text, as He will do on Holy Thursday and Good Friday in espousing His Church through the Last Supper and through the Crucifixion.

The Eucharist has been seen as the marriage feast of the Lamb. There is a nuptial content in this that must come and strike our hearts in this time. Because the question that this woman now asks of us is: Are we married single-heartedly to the one true God? Or are we, like her, having money, power, prestige and all kinds of other things as the real dominant forces of our living, but still holding on to the one true God on the side? We do that easily in real life. Spiritually, are we in an adulterous relationship with pleasure, with power, with prestige? Are we in an adulterous relationship, breaking faith with the one true God who we are covenanted to by the blood of His Son, Jesus Christ? That's at the very core of this gospel text as we face this terrible time in our world. We have to ask the very hard question: What is your faith? What is your faith in Jesus Christ? Are we in Christ and Christ alone, holding to Him and not letting go? Or are we holding to Christ and, also, holding to other things, hoping that these other things give us some form of life, not trusting that God and God alone will give us life? That is the hard question.

When the people went into exile, what happened was the house church became strong. While we are in exile – and that's where we are right now, we are in exile – my prayer is that the house church becomes very strong in whatever length of time we have to be away from public gatherings. For that to happen, we have to hear the question that the woman at the well is posing to every family right now: Have your children, have you, have your family been able to hold true to God and to God alone? Have you been able, not only to give them the faith that is your faith, but to bring them to the place where they have encountered God and they can say to you, "No longer do I believe because of what you say, but I believe because I believe! I have encountered Him and truly He is the Son of God!"?

As we enter into these days of desert, dryness, of fasting from the Eucharist, remember Hosea said, *"I will lead you back into the desert where, again, I will speak tenderly to your heart.*" The desert is the privileged space of God speaking to the hearts of the people to remind the people who their God truly is. And, in this desert time, God wants to remind us of who He really is, that He has paid the highest price for our relationship with Him and that price is the price of His Son given on the cross that you and I may have life. The blood of Jesus Christ is the price of the covenant, paid for you and for me. Let us see in these days of desolation, in these days of fasting like we've never fasted before, in these days of yearning for the Eucharist, in these days where we cannot participate as we usually would, let us see in this desert time a fast, a sacrifice, that would deepen and cleanse and purify our faith in Jesus Christ, that we will come out of this as from a refiner's fire, purified like gold and silver, but even purer than that.

This is a wonderful time, and this is a terrible time. It was the most difficult decision I have ever made as a bishop to say to this Church we cannot congregate for Mass. It was terrible! And it was difficult. And I made it, because I believed this is the decision that God asked of me to make. And I am asking you, as Church, that we use this time not to pull away into our frivolity, but to push back into our families, into our households and into our prayer. Let us make family prayer what we do in these days of desolation. Pick up your rosary. Remember we used to have this thing of the Family Rosary? Let us pull out the Family Rosary again and let us gather and pray the Rosary; let us open the scriptures and pray the scriptures. Let us pray together as a family and, in this time by this well where we are so thirsty, God will satisfy our thirst and He will give us living water that will flow up in us to eternal life. Amen.

No Prophet Is Accepted In His Own Country

Monday March 16, 2020.
Third Week of Lent.

First Reading: Second Kings 5: 1-15b
Responsorial Psalm: Psalm 42: 2-3; 43: 3-4
Gospel: Luke 4: 24-30
Homily: Archbishop Charles Jason Gordon

Our text today opens for us an intriguing way of thinking. In both our first reading and our gospel there is one theme that runs through: how do we see the action of God? What is required for God to convince us that He is acting? The Syrian Naaman, sent with letters and pomp and ceremony and a whole court of people, arrives at the prophet's house and the prophet does not even go out and meet him. He sends a servant to tell him to go and bathe in the Jordan. Now the Jordan River is mighty in our imagination because of the Baptism of Jesus but, the Jordan River was a very muddy little thing and it still is. The Syrian had these beautiful, magnificent rivers with clean water in his homeland so, of course, he was offended. Jesus had the same problem with His contemporaries. They had heard of all the miracles that He worked in other places. He comes now to His hometown, where He grew up, takes the scroll of the prophet Isaiah, reads from it and says, "These texts are being confirmed today and fulfilled even as you listen." And His people get angry with Him. Why? Sometimes, we want God to come in pomp, ceremony, majesty and a display of power. Sometimes, we want God to act in a mighty way, and God does that when He is ready – it's not that He can't. But many times God acts in very subtle, very small and very simple ways.

In the gospel, one of the problems they had with Jesus is the problem of the Incarnation. How could Jesus say that the text of the prophet is being fulfilled in their hearing? He is just a man: *"In fact, we know him. He is the carpenter is he not? We know his parents. We have known him since he was a child. How could he be claiming to be more than he actually is?"* And He says a prophet is only rejected in His own town. Sometimes, because we know people too well, we don't allow them to be everything God calls them to be. That is the challenge in our text today.

One of the commentaries on the text said something that shocked me: imagine if there was no Eucharist in the world today. Imagine if there was no Eucharist anywhere in the world and just one priest was alive in the world, and that one priest was celebrating the Eucharist. Would you not do everything you could to get yourself there to partake in the mystery? The point he was making is how often do we have the Eucharist present to us, and yet, how often do we approach it with such disdain, such lukewarmness? How often do we approach it without recognising what is really in our presence, because the bread looks like bread and the wine looks like wine? How often do we really recognise what we celebrate? Now that we are in the desert, now that there is this aridity, now that the Eucharist is not as present to us as it was before, many, many people have said to me how they yearn for God, how they yearn for the Eucharist and how this experience has taught them how precious a gift we have had, but not taken seriously.

The psalm today is a wonderful psalm: "O send forth Your light and Your truth." This psalm reminds us that in the little things – in the Eucharist, in your family member, in what we are doing in these days – God is present to us. I ask you today to remember that God is with us. We have determined that COVID means Christ Our Victory In the Desert, and in this desert to which we have been invited, Jesus Christ will be victorious. But we have to see Him in the little things of our daily existence. Do not do like Naaman and wish away the prophet because he asked for something simple. Do not do like the people of Nazareth and fail to see Jesus Christ because He comes in such a familiar disguise. Let us have the eyes of faith today that, in everything we do, we may see the God that is present to us in every single moment of every day. Let us have eyes of faith and let us pray for that in this Eucharist as we pray together. This Mass is being offered for every single person who participates by viewing. This Mass is offered for every one of you that our eyes may be opened, that we may see Christ in the little, and in the big, things of our lives. Amen.

PARABLE OF THE UNJUST SERVANT

Tuesday March 17, 2020.
Third Week of Lent.

First Reading: Daniel 3: 25, 34-43
Responsorial Psalm: Psalm 25: 4-5ab, 6 and 7bc, 8 and 9
Gospel: Matthew 18: 21-35
Homily: Archbishop Charles Jason Gordon

Our reading today really reminds me how awesome and funny God is. I mean, it's really like putting salt in a wound and rubbing it in. We have this wonderful prayer; the prayer is from the Book of Daniel and Azariah is standing in the midst of the fire. And, in the midst of this fire, he is begging God: *Remember Your people!* "Do not abandon us, O Lord for the sake of Your name; do not repudiate Your covenant with us, do not withdraw Your favour from us, for the sake of Abraham Your friend, and Isaac Your servant, and of Israel Your holy one." And then, he goes on to say: *"You know we have no leader, no prophet, no prince, no holocaust, no sacrifice, no oblation, no incense, no Mass, no communion, no gathering, no congregation – we have none of this, O Lord. I mean, oh gosh, Lord, I beg You, please, hear Your people, hear Your people!"*

The reading situates us in the same situation that Azariah felt and experienced when he was saying this prayer. He was in exile and, in exile, experienced the real wrath of the foreign nations against Israel and stood in the midst of the fire because he refused to bow to another god. And, because he refused to bow to the god of the nation where he was he was put into the fire, and in the fire he is there standing and praying to God. Have we refused to bow to the gods of the nations? Have we? Are we in the fire because we have been true to the living God? Have we refused to give in to the gods of power and money and wealth and pleasure and prestige? Or are we in the fire for a different reason? And that's the challenge our reading places on us today.

The people of the Exile understood that they were in exile because they had sinned, because they had done what was wrong, because they had disobeyed the covenant, because they had broken faith with God. They understood they were in exile because of that. You realise we are in exile? Do you realise that? We are in exile! We are not in the usual circumstance of our living. Lots of people are self-isolating. People are working in different ways. We don't have the connectivity that we used to have. The deepest human instinct in a time of trouble like this is to congregate, to come together, to support each other, to give consolation to each other in a physical, face-to-face way and this virus says we must not do that. Social distancing is the norm. But, as we are in exile through social distancing, self-isolation, as we are in exile, let us understand the logic of the exile. In the logic of the exile, several things are important. The first is that we have this opportunity to delve deeper into the heart of God. Now we have a whole lot of time that we didn't have before, you know? What are you doing with your time? Is it being filled with Netflix and WhatsApp and a whole lot of other things? Remember this is Lent, eh! Remember this God is so jokey He has given us COVID in Lent! What are we doing with our time? Prayer, fasting and almsgiving – that's what we're supposed to be doing. Let's not get distracted. Let's use this incredible opportunity of exile, of desert, and let us go deep into the Lenten practice, and let us understand that it is only when we go heart to heart with God that we will understand what God wants for His Church today.

Our gospel reading speaks about forgiveness. Poor Peter. Peter says, "Lord how often must I forgive my brother if he wrongs me? As often as seven times?" Now Peter thought he was doing a great thing, eh! Seven, you know, that's a big biblical number. Not seven, but seventy times seven. And the parable of forgiveness is the reminder to us that as we are in this exile, we are here in this desert, we are here for a reason and the reason is that we may learn how to forgive. So, I would ask you today to look again at your life, to meditate upon your life, to go deep today, deep, with all this extra time we have, because you can't go out this evening! With all this extra time we have, let's go deep today and let's really dig deep in our heart-to-heart with God. Let's have that conversation with God and let's ask God to show and to reveal to us the ways that we have kept Him as our God or the ways that we have made pact with the gods of money, the gods of pleasure, the gods of power, the gods of prestige. Let us also ask Him to show us who we need to forgive. Who do we need to forgive? Who have we held in our hearts? And, in this, let us recognise that this opportunity that we have is a wonderful moment for us because COVID, really and truly, is Christ Our Victory In the Desert. You got that one? C-O-V-I-D: Christ Our Victory In the Desert. In this desert we are in, Christ will be victorious, but He first must be victorious in my heart and in your heart. So, today, let us go into the desert and let us enter into this time with Christ. Let's put aside some of the time that we have to be with Him and let us enter deeply into that heart-to-heart with our God.

I Have Not Come to Abolish the Law or the Prophets.

Wednesday March 18, 2020.
Third Week of Lent.

First Reading: Deuteronomy 4: 1, 5-9
Responsorial Psalm: Psalm 147: 12-13, 15-16, 19-20
Gospel: Matthew 5: 17-19
HOMILY: Archbishop Charles Jason Gordon

Our readings today put something square and centre for us, and it's probably the hardest thing that a Trinidadian could deal with. And that is that the law is the law and it needs to be respected. You know, we are not really good with this at all, eh, you know that! You know, no matter how we try, we always think that we could do what we want with the law. But here's what is put before us today. Jesus says: "Not one dot, not one …stroke of the Law is going to disappear", because He hasn't come to abolish the Law, He's come to complete it. There are many people who believe that Jesus has abolished the Law and, therefore, now we could do as we want. Saint Augustine takes it to the next level and shows us how Jesus has completed the Law, because he says love and then do what you want, because if you love you will always do the loving thing and love will supersede the Law. The only way to live with the Law is to live in a moment that's higher than the Law.

In our first reading from Deuteronomy – such a wonderful text – Deuteronomy is setting out the whole Law for the people of Israel. And this Law that is being set out is undergirded by a truth: the truth that this God, who gives you the

Law, is a God of love. *"What people have a God so wonderful, so amazing, so powerful, as the God who gives you this Law today?* '…No other people are as wise and prudent as this great nation.' And, indeed, what great nation is there that has its gods so near as the Lord our God is to us whenever we call to Him? And what great nation is there that has laws and customs to match this whole Law that I have set before you today?"

When Jesus completes the Law, He takes it to the next level: *"You've heard how it was said an eye for an eye and a tooth for a tooth, but I say to you offer the wicked man no resistance."* It's not just that we don't give exact measure, it is that we go higher than that. *"You've heard how it was said do not commit adultery, but I say to you anyone who lusts has already broken the Law."* Jesus raises the bar. Why does He raise the bar? Because the Christian is not to live by the letter of the Law; the Christian is to live by the love of the God who has given us the Law, and to experience that love as the love that drives and determines everything in our life. And, so, when we live in this time where the government has asked certain things, when we live in this time where our freedoms have been restricted, when we live in this time where person-to-person contact is limited, we are asked to be very prudent with this. This is not how we normally live, but if we feel we can get away, not be caught, we do as we want. So, we throw a "Corona party", whereby we can congregate in somebody's house and nobody would know. This is something that we do! However, we take it to the next level: because we love Trinidad and Tobago, because we love God, because we love our neighbour, because we love the most vulnerable in this land, because we love those who are most at risk in this land, we do what we need to do in keeping social distance, physical distance, in practicing sanitation, in practicing hygiene. We do what we do because we love God.

There is a sense in our nation that we are above the law, that we could do what we want and skirt the law. And I would say that this is the greatest tragedy of Trinidad and Tobago. It has created the recklessness in our nation. It has allowed the corruption. It has allowed the high murder rate. It has allowed the flagrant breach of the law and total disregard for law. It has allowed an attitude amongst us that has created the licentiousness that we live at Carnival and during the year. It has allowed us to live without form and without definition. And, today, we have a reading in this season of Lent where we are led into this desert time, and this reading is speaking to the very soul of Trinidad and Tobago. We have to become a people, at the very least, who live by the law. But, at the most, live beyond the law because we live by the Law of Love. And therefore, not only will we not do the person-to-person contact, we will go beyond that to ensure that those in our community who are in need are taken care of. And rather than spending the time in dissipation and frivolity, let us make calls to our neighbours whom we know don't have support systems, and ensure that they are being cared for and looked after and loved. Let us ensure that the elderly have the groceries that they need, that they don't need to go out and expose themselves in this time.

There is the law and, then, there is the Law of Love. And what I put before you today is what Jesus put before His disciples and what Moses put before his community. We live within the law, but we live higher than that: we live the Law of Love and it is the Law of Love that calls us to love our neighbour. In Deuteronomy, the text is a summation of the "*Shema* Israel": "Love the Lord your God with all your heart, all your mind, all your soul." Jesus adds to that a summary of the Leviticus 19 text: "Love your neighbour as yourself." This is the whole Law that is set before you. And if we, in this desert period that we are living in, in this time of real difference for us in Trinidad and Tobago, if we could meditate on the truth of these readings today and how they speak to the soul of our nation and to all that has gone wrong in our nation, we will become a people who will again live the law, but who will again live higher than the law. We will live the Law of Love. Amen.

SAVIOUR OF THE SAVIOUR

ST. JOSEPH, HUSBAND OF MARY – Solemnity

Thursday March 19, 2020.
Third Week of Lent.

First Reading: Second Samuel 7: 4-5a, 12-14a, 16
Responsorial Psalm: Psalm 89: 2-5, 27 and 29
Second Reading: Romans 4: 13, 16-18, 22
Gospel: Matthew 1: 16, 18-21, 24a
HOMILY: Archbishop Charles Jason Gordon

Saint Joseph is a very important figure in our Church. He is a figure that has been underplayed for most of the life of the Church, but who has re-emerged over the last hundred, hundred and fifty years, and has steadily grown in importance. I would like to look at three dimensions of Joseph and his ministry and why he is an important saint.

The first is that he is the father of Jesus. When Jesus was a little boy growing up and He learnt to speak, He did not say "foster father"; he said "Papa", *"Abba"*. *"Abba"* is the Aramaic word for "Daddy" and, in saying *"Abba"*, He would have been saying something very important about His relationship with Joseph. Later, when Jesus would say: "My father keeps on working and so do I", He is referring both to Joseph and to His Father in heaven. Every time He speaks about the Father – as in the "Our Father": "Our Abba who art in heaven…" – His image for *"Abba"* would be Joseph. If you are a parent, I want you to imagine that, before your child was born, you knew you would not be around to take care of him, and you had to find somebody who would take care of your child. Who would you look for? What are the qualities of the person that you would choose? Somebody irresponsible? Somebody who may or may not take the responsibility seriously? Somebody who may or may not love him? You would look for the best person that you could find, not so? When God had to take care of His Son, Jesus Christ, who became flesh in the world, and God could choose from every man that lived, who did He choose? He chose Joseph, and by choosing Joseph He says something very special. Just as Mary was chosen to be the mother of God, Joseph was chosen to be the father of God and that realisation has been released in the Church very slowly over the last hundred and fifty years. The choice of Joseph was a deliberate one, particularly because of who he was.

First, he was the son of Jacob, but he was of the lineage of David. He was of the royal House of David and that is how Jesus is fulfilling the prophecy of Nathan to David, in the first reading today, that the lineage of David will last forever. Because Jesus is of the lineage of David, he is of the House of David and the prophecy is now fulfilled. As we experience the fulfilling of the prophecy because of Joseph, we must also recognise that if Joseph had said no in our gospel today – no to taking the child and His mother and being the father of Jesus – the prophecy would not be fulfilled, because Joseph gives something very significant: he gives his lineage, he gives Jesus the House of David. In the Jewish law, there is no such thing as foster father. A man chooses a child as his own, and that child has every right, every privilege, everything that a child of his blood would also have, and Joseph gives everything to Jesus. If God would choose Joseph to be father of Jesus, I think he must be a really, really good man.

Today, as we meditate on this time where we have gone into the desert, we have gone into this time of exile where there is no Church, no Mass, no Eucharist, no priest, no holocaust, no offering, I want us to think of another title that is being used for Joseph: "Saviour of the Saviour". Think of that title. The first time I heard it, it rocked me. Joseph is the Saviour of the Saviour! But not only is he Saviour of the Saviour, he is the only person who could claim this title. Not Mary, not any other human person, only Joseph has this title, "Saviour of the Saviour". It was to Joseph that God revealed in a dream: *"Take your wife, take your Child and take them down into the desert in Egypt."* It is Joseph who had the challenge of caring for the Child and the mother in the desert in Egypt. It is Joseph who provided for Him, it is Joseph who protected Him and it is Joseph who saved Him from Herod. If Joseph is the Saviour of the Saviour, I think we should be imploring him today, because if he understood how to get Jesus into safety from Herod, then he understands how to get the Church, which is the body of Christ, into safety from the modern Herod, which is the Coronavirus.

Remember, who is the first person that took care of the body of Christ? Joseph. Who is the first person who provided for Him? Joseph. Who is the first person that protected Him? Joseph. Who is the first person that saved Him? Joseph. If Joseph is Saviour of the Saviour, then Joseph is also our protector. In the 1860s, many people wrote asking the Holy Father, Pope Pius IX, to make Saint Joseph patron of the Church Universal. For years, people asked. A priest wrote to the Holy Father after prayer and fasting and he put in his letter: "Not only am I asking you to make Saint Joseph patron of the Church, Holy Father, I am giving my life for this cause and I offer myself as a victim sacrifice for this cause." When the Holy Father read that, two years later he made Saint Joseph Patron of the Church Universal. Why is Joseph Patron of the Church Universal? Because he is the patron of the body of Christ. He was the first patron of the body of Christ. When Christ was a little child, Joseph was His first protector, he was His first guide. Everything that Jesus learnt about prayer, about discipline, about work, about growing up, about manhood He learnt from Joseph. Today we are going to ask Joseph to be Patron of the Church Local, the Church in Trinidad and Tobago. We are inviting Joseph and asking him to protect us in this time where we are in Egypt, to protect us in this time where we are in the desert, to protect us in this time of peril.

O Joseph, as you protected the Boy and His mother from the perils of Herod and took them and put your mantle, your cloak, around them and protected them, we implore you today, O blessed Joseph, protect us this day. And put your mantle, put your cloak around the Church in this time again, that you may protect the body of Christ one more time, that you may protect us, the disciples of your Son, one more time, that you may spread your cloak, that you may protect us, that you may hold us and bring us safe again to God our Father. Amen.

THE FIRST OF ALL THE COMMANDMENTS

Friday March 20, 2020.
Third Week of Lent.

First Reading: Hosea 14: 2-10
Responsorial Psalm: Psalm 81: 6c-8a, 8bc-9, 10-11ab, 14 and 17
Gospel: Mark 12: 28-34
HOMILY: Archbishop Charles Jason Gordon

As I read that first reading my hearts breaks. My heart breaks because God is, literally, pleading with His people, pleading through the prophet that we return to Him: "Israel come back *to Me*, to the Lord your God; your iniquity was the cause of your downfall." This is the people in exile receiving a word from God through Hosea, and being begged, begged, "Come back to the Lord." Come back to the Lord.

The Book of Hosea is a very special book. The imagery at the heart of the book is the imagery of God as a jilted lover, God with "tabanca". God whose heart is broken because His beloved refuses to understand the radical extent of the love that God is pouring out to us, His people, and the beloved, that's us, are going off chasing other gods, other "husbands", and rejecting the One who loves us so completely and who has given everything for us. The imagery in the book speaks clearly to the relationship between God and His people, and it is not a relationship of chastisement or, even, of parent to child. It is a relationship of lovers and, on God's part, it is a relationship of a jilted lover who cannot contain His love any more and will do anything for the beloved to come back to Him.

We live in our exile, in our desert, and God is appealing to us: *"Come back to Me, come back to Me. ...* Your inequity was the cause of your downfall*." Come back to Me.* "Provide yourself with words and come back to the Lord. Say to Him, 'Take all our iniquity away so that we may have happiness again and offer You our words of praise.'" Then, He says, "I am like a cypress ever green, all your fruitfulness comes from Me. Let the wise man understand these words and let the intelligent man grasp their meaning; for the ways of the Lord are straight, and virtuous men walk in" His ways and do not stumble.

Have I really made God the centre and the all of my life? That is the question being asked of me from this text. Has God really been centre and all for me? Have I put other things as more important than God? Have I flirted with other gods, with power, with prestige, with possession, with pleasure, with all these other things that attract and are so alluring – have I flirted with that? Have I made those things more important than God and the intimacy to which He is calling me? In case we did not get the message from the first reading, the gospel gives us a way of responding to that first reading, in which we will know where we stand.

The scribe comes up to Jesus and puts the question, "Which is the first of all the commandments?" In the Jewish tradition, wherever there are two scripture passages that have the same words, they see them as connected at the hip even if they come from different parts of their scripture. What Jesus does is He connects two passages that have the same words. He connects the commandments, which is the *"Shema Israel"* – which every good Jew said three times a day – with Leviticus 19, which is, "You must love your neighbour as yourself." Love the Lord your God with every-thing – your mind, your heart, your understanding, your in-tellect, your will – and love your neighbour as yourself. These two are one, Jesus says, and He says this from within the Jewish tradition. The Jews would make that connection because the two texts have the same words in them, and these are the only two texts in the Old Testament that are connected in this way. Therefore, Jesus moves the Law to the next place, and if you want to know how we have moved away from God, well, we have it here. Do you love God with everything? With everything? Do you love God with all of you? And, if you say yes, well, maybe you are a saint here on earth already. Do you love your neighbour as you love yourself, or do you love yourself more than you love your neighbour? The second part is, you must love your neighbour as yourself. That means you must not put your neighbour before yourself, you must treat your neighbour as you would yourself. What you would want for yourself, you must want for your neighbour.

Here, we have the whole of the Law summarised for us. Here, we have the proof of how far we have gone from liv-ing what God has asked of us. Here, we have the call of re-pentance. Here, we have every reason to weep and to wail in our disgrace, because we have not loved God as God has invited us to love. God has given us more than what He gave to the prophet Hosea. In Hosea He used imagery, in the New Testament there is no imagery being used. He uses reality, and the reality of His love is the cross of Jesus Christ. It is His Son hanging on a cross. It is His Son who is given for us and giving everything, that you and I may know what the true intimate love of God is. Yes, this is an image of horror and torture, but it is also the image of true love. When a jilted lover still makes this sacrifice for the beloved, that is what real love looks like. In the face of this incredible love that has been poured out to you and me, I think you could make a better response. Actually, let me not speak for you; I think *I* could make a better response. What about you? Let us reflect, on this day, what response we are making to the Lord, to the incredible love that God has poured out to us, His children. Amen.

THE TAX COLLECTOR AND THE PHARISEE

Saturday March 21, 2020.
Third Week of Lent.

First Reading: Hosea 6: 1-6
Responsorial Psalm: Psalm 51: 3-4, 18-19, 20-21ab
Gospel: Luke 18: 9-14
HOMILY: Fr. Martin Sirju

My dear friends, last year I was present when we celebrated the birthday of one of our priests. It was in December, close to Christmas time, and we had one of the readings that speaks about St. Joseph. Day before yesterday, of course, was the Solemnity of St. Joseph, and that same passage popped up again. There was a woman at the birthday event – which was preceded by a little scripture sharing, Lectio Divina – and she said something very interesting regarding St. Joseph. She said, sometimes very good people do things that are not very nice. I found that was very insightful, because St Joseph is described as that devout and honourable man, that kind man, that loving man. Yet, sometimes as good people or very good people, we make mistakes; we do not make the best judgment at the time.

So, there was Joseph – a good man, an honourable man, a decent man – and, at some point, he was thinking of himself, his family, his friends and what they would say about his taking care of a child that is not his own. Then, he went into a dream, something happened and he changed his mind and became a better person. It shows that, even in the lives of good people, sometimes we make bad judgments but, thank God, we can always change our minds.

In today's gospel, we have before us, not a bad man – as many people think – but a good man and this man is not a Scribe or a Sadducee. He is a Pharisee, which means that he belongs to the more progressive movement of Judaism at the time. They were at the forefront of reinterpreting the scriptures, so he represents a very progressive body in the eyes of his people. In addition to that, we can learn something about him from how he prays.

He starts off by saying that he gives thanks. Often, when we pray, instead of giving thanks we ask for all sorts of things. I have this little funny experience when I was parish priest in Siparia. On Holy Thursday, thousands of people would come and honour the statue of Our Lady known as La Divina Pastora or *"Sipari Mai"*: Hindi for "Siparia Mother". I was told this man ended up in front of the statue of La Divina Pastora and he said, "What do I do?" They said to him, "Well, ask for want you want". He said, "Okay, give me house, give me car, give me land, give me money," and he started asking for everything. Today's gospel tells us that the Pharisee does not start off by asking for anything for himself, but by giving thanks.

It also tells us that he pays tithes on all he gets; is that something that we do? Are we faithful to our collection, our portion that we give for the ongoing ministry of the Church? At Christmas, for instance, I think people probably spend a lot on what they want and what they would like to enjoy and, afterwards, then they say, "Okay, I will give what is left back in my collection to the Church." One of my colleagues living with me, Father Martin, told his parishioners, "I am sure that the average man who comes to church, when he was goes to lime he might have two, three beers – that's $30 right there. What do you give to your Church?" Do you pay your tithes? The Pharisee says this morning very openly to God, "I pay tithes on all I get," which is something many of us cannot say.

He also says, "I fast twice a week." Do we fast at all? We have gone to the other extreme of spiritualising fasting: fasting from gossip, fasting from impatience, fasting from always wanting to have my say. But, the physical fast remains and he says, "I fast twice a week." Our usual days are Wednesdays and Fridays but, particularly outside of Lent, we have TGIF – "Thank God It's Friday". Friday is a liming day, but Friday remains a penitential day in the life of the Church. He recognises that; he says, "I fast twice a week." This is something Our Lady has been saying to us way back since the 19th century when we had this splurge of apparitions. Also, for the past thirty-something years in Medjugorje, she has been saying the same thing: "Fast." He says to God, "I fast twice a week"; that is something for us to reflect on, as well.

So where did this good man go wrong? This good man went wrong when, because of his religious activity, he starts to look down upon others and think that he is better than them. If I might say, this is really clericalism. It is not just the sin of the Pharisee, but it is a sin of which people like myself – priests, bishops and so on – sometimes become guilty. Clericalism; there is something in us that makes us think, "I am 'better than'". Or, even as a lay person, "I am better than this one", and this is where he goes wrong. Jesus, in this parable, compares him to the tax collector who is sincerely repentant, who beats his breast and says: "God be merciful to me, a sinner."

St. Augustine said that a repentant sinner, a repentant prostitute, will get into the kingdom of heaven faster than an arrogant virgin. It is all about our hearts, the kind of heart we bring before God, and this man brought his heart before God this morning in the temple, beating his breast and praying more sincerely than the Pharisee prayed. Let us also remember Pope Francis' caution to us in his message for the World Day of Peace, that we must not be afraid of the other. There is some hidden fear as he looks down upon this man, as if he would be, maybe, contaminated by him and there is that fear of those who are different or those who are perceived to be unrepentant sinners or just sinners. But, our hearts ought to be different.

We give God thanks this morning that the gospel passage speaks to us and calls us to go deeper in this season of Lent, to not pray only from our heads but from our hearts and, also, to see the other not as the enemy, not as somebody I am "better than", but a pilgrim with whom I am called to journey, to give thanks and to build up God's Kingdom on earth.

FOURTH WEEK OF LENT

HEALING OF THE MAN BORN BLIND

Sunday March 22, 2020.
Fourth Sunday of Lent.

First Reading: First Samuel 16: 1b, 6-7, 10-13a
Responsorial Psalm: Psalm 23: 1-3a, 3b-4, 5, 6 (1)
Second Reading: Ephesians 5: 8-14
Gospel: John 9: 1-41
HOMILY: Archbishop Charles Jason Gordon

Our reading today is one of those texts that is so big, so huge, so gigantic that I am afraid that if I am really to do justice to this text, we would be here until late tonight. So, we going to do with the text what we do; to understand this text is to understand it has a context. So, although this is John 9, you have to go back to John 7 and see that the people were all gathered in Jerusalem because of the Feast of Tabernacles. The Feast of Tabernacles is a feast where the people of God come to Jerusalem, they build some little tents and they all live in their own tents during this feast to remind themselves that, for forty years, the people of God lived in tents while they were in the desert. Does that sound familiar to anybody? Huddled in small spaces? Remember we are in the desert; any connection yet?

So, this is the context: they are in Jerusalem for this Feast of Tabernacles, which is just finished. They are saying, "We are the disciples of Moses," because Moses is the one who led the people through the desert and through this difficult time in their lives. We are in the desert and wherever you call your house is now the tabernacle; it is now a tent. It is now a meeting place. It is now a place of indwelling, because we are all huddled in our Jerusalem over the next while. Let's pray it is only for forty days. Let's pray but, however long it is, that's where we are. In the reading, as they would have gone through this Feast of Tabernacles, they would have remembered the works of God in the desert. They would have remembered that it was in the desert that Moses struck the rock and water flowed out – hence, our reading from last week about the woman at the well and the waters of eternal life. They would have remembered that in the desert they were hungry and God fed them with manna. And they would have also remembered how they complained about the bread, "This bread is unsatisfying, give us real food to eat!" That should remind every Catholic, every single one of us, of the many complaints we have had about the Eucharist being unsatisfying, as being food that has not sustained us, now that we are having a fast from the Eucharist. We should remember all the ways that we thought it unsatisfying; remember all the many Catholics who have left the Church because they did not understand the significance of the Bread of Life and how this is real food.

We are in our desert, and it is in the desert that God led the people to true faith. That's what the whole reading in our gospel is about – coming to the light of faith. In this reading, we have a man who was born blind, and we see in this man a type of the whole human race. Typology is a tool that biblical writers use very often. It is a metaphor, an image of something much bigger, much more profound than what is presented, an image of a sacred Mystery that cannot easily be contained. In this text, we have a type appointed to the sacred Mystery which is Baptism, and it leads us through all the steps towards baptism, the steps through which we come to faith in God. And so, as we go through the reading, I want you to reflect on your own baptism.

Do you know when you were baptised? Do you remember? No? Most of us were babies brought by our parents, but the significance of our baptism is so important, so let us go through the reading and reflect on its significance. You see the man was born blind and they asked, "Who sinned, him or his parents?" Jesus said neither he nor his parents sinned, but he was made so that the glory of God may be revealed. That is true of every human person ever born, because we are born blind, every single one of us. Blinded by Original Sin, blinded by concupiscence, blinded by our inability to understand who God is, blinded because Adam and Eve disobeyed and that sin of concupiscence and Original Sin passed right down to you and to me. Therefore, we have this disordered affection for sin, this movement in our soul towards what is wrong and this is what is overcome through the grace of baptism and through the grace of Christ-like living that fills our whole being. What we now have in our text is a type of the whole human family, because we were born blind. But we were born blinded by Original Sin, so that the glory of God may be revealed and seen by all. So, for this man who now stands for the whole human race, Jesus does something most amazing: He bends down and starts to make some clay on the ground – the actual word used here is "clay" in the Greek. He makes clay using dust and spittle, then takes this clay and rubs it on the man's eyes.

Now, we have to remember that this, for first-century Jews, would be seen differently to the way we see it today. In the text just before this one, we have Jesus saying: "Before Abraham ever was, I AM." He invokes the name that God revealed to Moses: the great "I AM" and, so claims to be God. Having claimed to be God, He is now making clay and performing miracles. You see, in the beginning, on the first day God said, "Let there be light" and there was light, and we saw how the light illumed the darkness. Then, God took the clay, formed it, fashioned it, breathed on it and brought it into life. As a living human being, Jesus is acting as a Divine One: making the clay, putting it on the blindness of the man's eyes and regenerating his sight, giving new sight. Why? Because in the Garden, they ate the fruit because they wanted to see.

They wanted the wisdom, for their eyes to be opened, to see, to know as God does. But, rather than their eyes being opened, their eyes were closed to God and open only to seeing themselves, and that's how they knew they were naked. So, rather than coming to wisdom and insight and clarity of sight, they came to blindness because all they could see was themselves and their own nakedness. Now God is opening the eyes of the blind that were shut by sin with Adam and Eve, and this opening of the blind eyes means that we now can see God. We see that echoed by the disciples at Emmaus, "when their eyes were opened and they recognised them in the breaking of the bread".

So, this theme of blindness and sight is a theme that starts in Genesis. It is a theme in the very soul of Creation, but is in the very soul of the Redemption brought to us in Jesus Christ. As we experience this theme of blindness and sight, we return to the man who is offered sight. After Jesus applies the clay, He instructs the man, "Go and wash in Siloam." We are told the name "Siloam" means "sent"; the man goes and washes and now he can see. In Baptism, we start with the anointing, then the washing, and then the re-generation of faith happens. So the very things that Jesus is doing for the man is exactly what is done in Baptism: an anointing and a washing leading to faith.

Let's look at the journey the man makes; you see the man moving in one direction and the Pharisees moving in the opposite. The Pharisees start out divided, some saying, *"Maybe he is a good man, in truth, because, I mean, only good men could do good things. A bad man can't do good things."* But they end up expelling the man from the syna-gogue and from the community, excommunicating him be-cause he believes that Jesus is a man of God. They start off with an open mind and end up in absolute blindness.

This man, on the other hand, starts off blind and ends up with incredible sight! The journey of the man is wonderful! Remember, he was blind so he didn't see anything: didn't see the paste being made, didn't see the paste being put on his eyes – nothing. All he knew was, that when he washed in Siloam, his eyes were opened and he could see. So even if Jesus stood in front of him, he would not have recognised Jesus. The encounter between him and Jesus is so wonder-ful! When he is first asked to, "Give glory to God, tell us what happened," he said, *"Well, I don't know. There was a man, His name was Jesus, He put a paste and send me to Siloam and now I can see."* The text has so much irony and humour in it; the next time they asked him, he said, *"So, what? You want to be a disciple or what? What you asking so much questions about this man for? You, too, want to follow Him?"* No, "We are the disciples of Moses." Remember: Feast of Tabernacles, desert? The man now comes to another place. They ask, *"Who is He?"* He says, *"He must be a prophet, because only a prophet can do things like this."* The third time they ask about Jesus, the man says: *"Well, He has to be a man of God, because only a man of God can act this way, because people who are not of God could not do this. It has never been heard that a man born blind had his eyes opened."*

Now, we must remember Luke who says, quoting Isaiah: "The spirit of the Lord is upon me; He sent me to bring good news to the poor, to open the eyes of the blind and to set the captives free." Because here, the man is witnessing to the faith he now has in Jesus Christ. Remember, he has only met Him once and, now, at the end of this epic story, when he meets Jesus, Jesus says to Him, "Do you believe in the Son of Man?" Now, every first-century Jew would know the "Son of Man" is a designation given in the Book of Daniel and was a title of God, of the Messiah who is coming, and the whole community was waiting on this Messiah. "Do you believe in the Son of Man? *Do you believe in the Messiah?*" The man says, "Show me who He is so that I may believe in Him." *"I who Am speaking to you; I Am He."* And the man does two things: he says, "Lord, I believe", accepting Jesus as Lord, as God. Then, he bows down and worships Him, and this is what the whole Mystery of Baptism is about – that we come to bow down and to worship this man. We understand that Jesus is not just a man, not just a prophet, not just a man of God, He is the Messiah and that means our whole life is configured through His word to us, and we now live for Him. This man bows down and worships Jesus and, in worshipping Him, comes to true faith in God.

Jesus plays with blindness and sight. When the Pharisees hear Him talk about blindness and sight, they say, *"Wait, you think we are blind?"* And, He responds, *"You know, if you said you were blind, then you would be okay, you know. But, because you say you could see, the penalty on you is even greater, because judgment will come into the world and those who believe they have sight and are blind, they are even more blind."* Our text says something else. For the last thirty years, certainly the last twenty years from 2000 until now, where the Church has been embattled by so many scandals and difficult times, it has been easy to ridicule the Church and to ridicule the things of the Church, so easy to look at the Church as passé, as an institution that has died. When Pope John Paul II died, the whole Church believed it was the end of the Church. When Pope Benedict resigned, the whole Western media believed the Church had come to its end. When Pope Francis began, everybody understood that the Church was the institution that God intended Her to be. The whole opinion changed – that is the difference between the opinion of the world and the opinion of faith.

These days when we are living in our tabernacles – yes, shut in houses where we are hungering for the Bread of Life because we cannot receive it and understand now how precious this bread is, where we just don't know what to do any more, when we are hungering for all the Mysteries of God and the Sacrament of Reconciliation and so many things – let us pray that our eyes may be opened to see God again.

And that we may see, in the mystery of this time, the God who is life. *"Who has sinned to make this COVID virus so terrible?"* Maybe, just so the glory of God may be revealed. Maybe that's why we are experiencing what we are experiencing. But my challenge and request to you as individuals and as families: make a list of the things that you need to be grateful to God for; make a list, write it down – mysteries in your life, the joys, the blessings you have received, your family, the sunshine, a sunrise, a sunset, the relationships you have. Make a list and include the mysteries of God that we receive through the Church of which we are most appreciative. Make a list and let us be like this man, giving glory to God for the wonderful things God has done for us. And maybe, in our gratitude, our eyes may be opened to the truth of a God who has always been with us, a God who is with us right now, right here in this moment, in this time and in this place.

Let us pray that the blindness which we have lived may be changed to true sight, and the Light who came into the world to enlighten all, the true Light, may enlighten our eyes and our minds because we live by faith and not by sight. It is only Jesus Christ who can give us this faith. Let us pray for the gift of faith today for ourselves and for our families, that this faith may well up to the source of eternal life and bring us to our knees to worship this God. Amen.

HEALING OF THE COURT OFFICIAL'S SON

Monday March 23, 2020.
Fourth Week of Lent.

First Reading: Isaiah 65: 17-21
Responsorial Psalm: Psalm 30: 2 and 4, 5-6, 11-12a and 13b
Gospel: John 4: 43-54
HOMILY: Archbishop Charles Jason Gordon

In the midst of this coronavirus season – where we are faced with such death, difficulty, negativity, so many things coming at us, holding us in such terrible fixation on all that is going round, the whole world tottering on the brink of disaster, in all of this – the Lord is close, smiling on us today with these readings of hope, readings that are speaking about a new beginning. The prophet Isaiah says: "Now I create new heavens and a new earth, and the past will not be remembered and will come no more to men's minds." Wow! "I create new heavens and a new earth..."

What we are now experiencing is re-creation – the pangs of birth, the pain of labour. God is creating something, He is creating something new! If we want to be part of this new creation then we have to see, in this time, where the hand of God is. And we have to respond through faith to the hand of God – the desire of God, the work of God, the invitation of God – to be part of this new creation, part of this new heaven, part of this new earth.

We know the old creation, our life before three weeks ago, was not at its best – I am trying to be as diplomatic as possible! It was not at its best. It was not the life that God wanted for us, it was not living in the manner that God desired. It was not doing the intimacy with God in the way God wanted, or the intimacy with each other. We weren't as caring with each other, we weren't building families of faith because we were distracted by so many things. Since we've had to shut down everything and we now have to come back to a way of living that we have not had for many, many years, and since families are now home and people are having more time together, how do we help God in this new creation? Well, what about family prayer? Everybody is home now; what about Family Rosary, what about gathering around the Bible? What about talking about the things that we are grateful for? Remember, yesterday, I asked you to make a list? Well, what about sharing that list around the table with your family, about the gratitude you have to God for the many ways that God has blessed you?

If we do what God is intending and asking during this time, when this time of coronavirus is ended we will see a new heaven and a new earth. We will see a new civilisation emerge, we will see family life in a different way and we will see new opportunities for hope and faith and praise and love and life. We will see a better Trinidad and Tobago and we will see a better Catholic Church. But if, during this time, we do all the things we are accustomed to doing and we are not turning to Him and crying, then at the end, we will have the same hell that we had before we went into this.

In our gospel reading, we see the man from Capernaum pleading earnestly with Jesus to heal his child. And, having experienced the miracle of God, the man and his whole household praised God – this whole household! They believed and they praised God. The invitation for us, today, is to beg on behalf of your family. To plead with God, on behalf of your family, for grace, for conversion, for the family coming back to God in a brand-new way.

As we come to this Eucharist today, remember I am offering the Eucharist for you – for your prayers, your intentions. Remember that, and remember on this altar today, as I raise the host and the chalice, I raise you and I bring you and your family before God and ask God to do a new thing, that He will create a new heaven and a new earth and you will be part of this new creation.

Let us pray.

HEALING OF THE SICK MAN AT BETHZATHA

Tuesday March 24, 2020.
Fourth Week of Lent.

First Reading: Ezekiel 47: 1-9, 12
Responsorial Psalm: Psalm 46: 2-3, 5-6, 8-9
Gospel: John 5: 1-3a, 5-16
HOMILY: Archbishop Charles Jason Gordon

You know I love the Church's readings! I love how they work and I love how they feed us and I love how they challenge us. I love how they move us along in this middle time of Lent where we are experiencing this desert – arid, arid land. Remember Lent is this desert time into which we have been plunged for these forty days.

In our first reading from the prophet Ezekiel, the angel takes the prophet up to the high mountain – that's up to the temple, to the parapet of the temple – and he says, "Look eastwards." Now if you are up in the parapet of the temple and you look eastwards, what you see is the Kedron Valley of the Mount of Olives. Then, if you look in the distance behind that, what you will see is the Dead Sea – that's the sea that has no life; nothing lives in it, nothing lives around it. Rich in minerals, but zero in life. It brings life to nothing; it is absolutely dead. And, then, we have this reading saying that, from this temple, from the heart of the temple, flows a stream. And as the stream is flowing, an angel measures out a thousand cubits and has Ezekiel wade through it; he does, and his feet get wet. Then the angel measures out another thousand cubits; Ezekiel wades across it again and it is now up to his thighs. Wades in it again and it is up to his waist.

Wades in it again... and the angel keeps measuring out more and more and, with each measuring, the water gets higher and higher. This is an image of faith; this is what faith is.

In our first encounter with faith, we wade through the stream: the waters of Baptism. And in the waters of Baptism, we come to faith, but it's just a little trickle at this stage. As we go to the next stage and make a conscious choice to be a disciple of Jesus Christ, where we make His word our home, make His command our life's call and seek out vocation, then the water is now up to the thighs. As we wade a little more into this river of faith, we come to that place where we are missionary disciples and we want to give our life to Christ. We are now ready to bring the Good News to other people, ready for the hardships of the gospel. We are ready to be generous with our lives, giving our talent and treasure to God, no longer counting cost and time. We are being generous, having experienced God's generosity to us because now the water is up to our waist and we are experiencing a fullness of this love. Measure out again, now the water is over our head – that's the mystical union with Christ. That's when we and Christ become one: "I am in you and you are in Me." "Abide in Me as I abide in you." This is the ultimate call of every Christian, to enter into mystical union with their God. This is the apex of the Christian call and this is what the prophet is measuring out – the different stages of development of Christian faith.

Where are you along this journey of faith? Where are you? Just water to your ankles? Or already turned to go further as a disciple or a missionary disciple or, ultimately, to mystical union with God? And hear what the reading says: as the river swells it brings life to the Dead Sea. It brings life to that sea that had no life in it at all: fish start teeming in it and, on the banks, trees are growing and the leaves of these trees are medicinal. Whoever wades into the water finds life – that's what happens to the soul when we give ourselves completely to our God: the desert turns to a fertile field and the dry land becomes a wilderness with incredible life teeming in it, and the "Dead Sea" that could give no life is transformed into life-giving water, welling up to eternal life inside of us.

This is the promise of Jesus Christ in the midst of this COVID desert in which we are living. Do not stop short on the early stages of faith. So many of us have hovered with our ankles in the water, stepping back on to dry land. Do not be satisfied by just touching faith lightly. This is the moment, in the midst of this desert, to wade in the water. Wade deep into this water, because God is troubling up the water to teem with life inside of us that we will bring life to everyone we touch; this is the living water that He speaks about. This is life; this is the Christ-like thing we speak about. I invite you today to see where you are in your journey of faith; measure out the next cubit and delve deeper and deeper into this life-giving water into which Christ is inviting you.

HE WILL BE CALLED
SON OF THE MOST HIGH

ANNUNCIATION OF THE LORD – Solemnity

Wednesday March 25, 2020.
Fourth Week of Lent.

First Reading: Isaiah 7: 10-14; 8: 10
Responsorial Psalm: Psalm 40: 7-8a, 8b-9, 10, 11
Second Reading: Hebrews 10: 4-10
Gospel: Luke 1: 26-38
HOMILY: Archbishop Charles Jason Gordon

Some years, God gives us a little "bligh", a little ease, during Lent. In the midst of this Lenten period we have two solemnities; this is one of them. We had St. Joseph on the 19th of March and today, the 25th of March, we have the Annunciation. In this celebration, we are celebrating something that is really powerful, very profound. What we are celebrating is that God made a choice to break the silence and, in breaking the silence, what He does is open a new way for us, His people.

In the Genesis story, Adam and Eve closed the door to Paradise, effectively, closing off our communion with God, the intimacy where we walked with God in the cool of the evening; that was undone through the sin of Adam and Eve. One sin, and we all pay the consequences.

What we have here, in the Annunciation, is the dawn of salvation history – the first light to be lit after Adam and Eve closed the portal, the relationship with God. Mary's yes opens back that portal to grace, that intimacy with God. In this move, where God sends the angel to this woman called Mary in Nazareth, what we have is God offering salvation, once again, for you and for me. And, in offering this salvation, what we have is something unprecedented: Abraham longed to see this day, David longed to see this day, all the prophets and patriarchs hoped to see the day when God would send His Messiah, but none could have imagined that the Messiah would come as a baby, born true God, true man. What we have is Mary's yes: "Let it be done to me according to Thy word. And, the angel left her."

You know, this is the greatest gamble in history; the absolute, greatest gamble! The last time God did this – Adam and Eve – look what happened! Look how bad that went! But He takes a second chance; He gives humanity a second chance, saying to Mary, "If you say yes, the whole world will change!" The gamble is also Mary's gamble, because if Mary says yes and Joseph disowns her, she could be stoned to death. So Mary, herself, pays a high price in this new dispensation. Eve's no closed off salvation history, Mary's yes opens it up again and, now, you and I have choices to make. Will we be children of Eve or children of Mary? The Annunciation invites a new lineage, because Mary is the new Eve and this new Eve gives birth to a new humanity, and this new humanity is a humanity that constantly says yes to God. To be part of the lineage of Mary is to be part of the lineage that says yes to God.

Today, I would like you to reflect on what are you saying to God. When God proposes, when God asks, when you are clear about what God is inviting you to, are you saying no and being a child of Eve, or are you saying yes and being a child of Mary? Mary's yes allowed God to act in this world; our yes and our no also allow or inhibit God's action in the world. There is a wonderful sermon by St. Bernard of Clairvaux in which he says that, when the angel visited Mary and asked her to be the mother of Jesus, Adam and Eve waited in hushed breath, waiting to hear the answer of the Virgin. Abraham and all the Patriarchs, they waited. The prophets waited, all those in Sheol whose life had been condemned – they, too, waited to hear. The heavenly court was in hushed silence, waiting. And God, Himself, waited.

"'Let it be done according to Thy word.' And the angel left her." And, every moment of every day, God is waiting with bated breath to see what you will say: yes or no. Will you be a child of Mary or a child of Eve? As we come to celebrate this incredible moment, where God again proposes to humanity that He take us back and sends His Son as one of us, in this moment, you and I find a challenge to how we have been living. Do you say yes, or do you say no? In every moment we answer God and, in every moment, we make decisions either to become the best or the worst version of ourselves. Today let us ask Mary's intercession that we will constantly say yes to God and become the person God has asked us to be. Amen.

REFUSAL TO BELIEVE IN CHRIST

Thursday March 26, 2020.
Fourth Week of Lent.

First Reading: Exodus 32: 7-14
Responsorial Psalm: Psalm 106: 19-20, 21-22, 23
Gospel: John 5: 31-47
HOMILY: Archbishop Charles Jason Gordon

Well, yesterday we had a little reprieve, you know. We had that Feast of the Annunciation, which broke the rhythm of Lent. And just in case we forget where we are, we are in the desert, we are in this time of testing, being tested in so many different ways! The testing and the desert – not only the Lenten testing and desert, but also the COVID testing and desert and, in this, what we are having now is a reading that is asking a very difficult question – one of the tough ones.

Moses had been up Mt. Sinai, and up in Mt. Sinai the whole glory of God was displayed. God wrote the Law on two tablets and handed them to Moses as His covenant with His people. The covenant is the betrothal – the marriage between God and His people. These Ten Commandments are how the community will be directed. But, before Moses can leave the mountain and return to the people, the people had already walked away from God. He didn't even get down the mountain! You know it is a funny little piece of scripture when Moses saw Aaron, who was the priest. He says: *"Aaron how could you do this?"* and Aaron said, *"It's not me, you know! They have some gold there and I threw it into the fire and a calf came out."* Well, really, isn't that what we do? Not take responsibility? So, let's ask now about the idols and speak to the idols that exist.

Here is the command from God, the First Commandment: "You must have no other God before Me." Can we really say that God is God first and only? Can we really say that, or have we put other things before God? Do we use our time thinking about God first or do we use our time such that God kinda fits in if we have some time left over? Do we use our money thinking about God first and ask, "How would God want me to spend this money that I have?" Or do we spend our money, and fit God in somewhere after?

When it comes to prestige and people recognising us, all the likes on Facebook, people tweeting and responding on WhatsApp, Instagram and all the other social media, when it comes to that, do we put God first or do we seek the approval of everyone else first? Do we push what we do to seek approval from other people, rather than being messengers of God first? Ideology comes in many ways. In the Old Testament, it was a physical form – a golden calf which they worshipped. In our modern times, the idols aren't physical; many people are worshipping pleasure. Do we often make choices for pleasure that we know are wrong? Do we put our choice for pleasure before our choice for God? Where are we? Is God really the God of our life? Is God really first and foremost in everything in our life?

The second piece of this scripture is so beautiful. Moses is now on the back foot, defending the people and saying to God, *"You know, Lord, for the sake of this people, for Abraham, for Isaac, for Jacob, for all of these people, for all of our ancestors, for the sake of them, please be merciful to these people. How it go look? You know You brought them out of Egypt. You brought them through the desert to kill them? You know that's what everybody's going to say!"* Moses defends the people, interceding on their behalf, and he can do so because he is a friend of God. We are called now to intercede on behalf of our families, children, grandchildren, great-grandchildren. We are called to intercede on behalf of God for them, especially if we see that they are not living as God has asked us to live, especially if we recognise they have not put God first.

Moses interceded for his people, you are called to intercede for your people, I am called to intercede for my people, and you are my people and that's why every day I am offering Mass for your intentions. That's why every day I am praying that your journey with God will deepen and deepen and deepen as we go through this desert together. The reading is a heart-breaking reading because everything that God showed in love to the people, they rejected, yet God was merciful, God was kind.

The text right after this one is one of the most beautiful texts because it speaks about a God of mercy and kindness and tenderness who forgives to the next generation, whose love is always supreme. Today, as we hear the word of God, as we hear the word of God, I ask you to spend some time today asking yourself: Is God really first in my life? Have I made God, God? Or have I put other things as god and then fit God in wherever I could? Today let us return to the Lord with all of our hearts, that our whole being would put God first, that God will be our God. Amen.

CLAIMING TO KNOW JESUS' ORIGIN

Friday March 27, 2020.
Fourth Week of Lent.

First Reading: Wisdom 2: 1a, 12-22
Responsorial Psalm: Psalm 34: 17-18, 19-20, 21 and 23
Gospel: John 7: 1-2, 10, 25-30
HOMILY: Archbishop Charles Jason Gordon

Our reading today really paints a great picture. In our first reading from the Book of Wisdom, we have this reflection where the ungodly are seeking to do harm to a person who is virtuous. Why would that happen? The ungodly don't just leave him alone and say, *"Well, he thinks he's virtuous, let him go."* No, they physically seek to do harm to him *because* he is virtuous. They say: "Let us wait for the virtuous man since he annoys us and opposes our way of life."

The ungodly is affected by the virtuous person, and that leads to anger, jealousy, to violence. That's the heart of this reading: the godliness of a person – closeness to God, living the virtuous life, seeking to do what is right because it is right regardless of the consequences – affects people. It affects people and because it affects people violence, jealousy, rage and all kinds of negative reactions come.

The readings are given to us today to help us understand why Jesus Christ is going to be crucified, though He was innocent and sinless. We heaped the violence of the world on top of Him. Why? Because, as we read in the first reading, He affected their way of life. He challenged, to the core, the way that they were living. He put in clear light, the blindness that they were holding to and because, unconsciously, the virtuous is affecting the ungodly, the virtuous now becomes the target of the ungodly.

Let us reflect on that for a little bit. Have you ever been in a situation, where you have stood for what is right, done the noble thing and because of that had people against you? Really against you? I mean in a most bizarre way that becomes irrational! Have you ever experienced that? Now what about the opposite? Have you ever become irrationally angry at somebody simply because they did something that made you feel uncomfortable, because they held the right line, because they did the right thing, because they challenged all of the mediocrity? And rather than stepping up and growing, you joined the bandwagon of shaming, of naming-calling and of discrediting. Have you ever been on that side of this equation? Because that, too, is the drama of the crucifixion – that is the drama of it. The reading says: "This is the way they reason, but they are misled. Their malice makes them blind. They do not know the hidden things of God, they have no hope that holiness will be rewarded, they can see no reward for blameless souls." Holiness will be rewarded; living a righteous life will be rewarded. It will create havoc here on earth for many people, but it will be rewarded. Many people will object, but the holy life is the life that has the most impact in our world. Think of Jesus Christ: who has had more impact than Jesus Christ? Who? And who has received more anger, more negativity, more taunts, more rejection than Jesus Christ? So, His holiness was rejected, but the impact of His life lasts to today and will last beyond today to the end of time. From this perspective, I want to encourage you today to see again, to listen again, to hear again that call to holiness, that call to live a virtuous life, that call to dedicate yourself to God, that call to give yourself to Him. And, wherever you are in the spectrum of the godly or ungodly – those who have been for, and helping, and aiding the virtuous man or those who have been against – every one of us today can recognise ourselves in the drama of the crucifixion, and that's what has been put before us on this Friday in Lent.

The drama of the crucifixion, this is the inner logic of why Christ was crucified and we are entering into the drama. As we look at our nation, we are invited into this drama and what a drama we have! At this time, we could choose to live in a most ungodly way or we could choose to live in a most godly way. We could choose to be neighbourly, we could choose to be helpful to those in need, we could choose to check up on those in the community who are in need – the lonely, the sick, the elderly. We could choose to ensure that we are our brother's or sister's keeper, we could choose to do the right thing, we could choose to stop as a family and pray every day, we could choose to put our fear and anxiety aside and recognise that God is in charge. We could choose to move away from the panic and centre ourselves in God and know that God will see us through this.

These are choices that we can make. As we listen to the readings today and we see in the first reading and the gospel this drama of anger towards the godly, we could choose to be Simon of Cyrene, or we could choose to be Veronica, or we could choose to be the mob, soldiers or Pilate. We are invited to the drama of the crucifixion. Enter into it and choose which side of this drama you want to be part of. Amen.

THE CHRIST COULD NOT BE FROM GALILEE

Saturday March 28, 2020.
Fourth Week of Lent.

First Reading: Jeremiah 11: 18-20
Responsorial Psalm: Psalm 7: 2-3, 9bc-10, 11-12
Gospel: John 7: 40-53
HOMILY: Fr. Martin Sirju

My dear friends, in the infant baptism rite, at the end, there is a little rite called the Ephphatha Rite, in which the priest takes his thumb and marks the ear of the child, then the other ear and, then, he takes his thumb and signs the lips with the Sign of the Cross. The rite is actually called that: the Ephphatha Rite. It is really derived from the adult preparation for baptism rite and would have been done in the Rite of Acceptance. In the Rite of Acceptance, the senses are signed so the candidate to be baptised is signed on the forehead, on the eyes, on the mouth, on the ears, on the heart, on the shoulders and so on. What is all that about? That is to indicate that to become a Christian, to follow Christ as a disciple, we give everything to Christ.

Everything belongs to Him and all parts of our being must be open to Him. So, openness is a very important spiritual quality. The opposite of that openness is a hardness of heart which leads to blindness. Today's gospel links us with the gospel of last Sunday, which covered the story of the man born blind. The irony of the story is that the man born blind can see and the other people – the neighbours, the crowds, the Pharisees – are the ones who cannot see. They cannot see; therefore, they are blind, and they cannot see because

81

they are not open. We see the same thing in this morning's passage from the Gospel of Saint John. The Pharisees, because they are not open, do not see. Because they do not see, they do not come to faith in Christ. But other people see, and they come to faith in Christ because they are open. And so, we have in the gospel passage, the Pharisees becoming angry, saying, "This rabble knows nothing of the Law." And then, a little later on, when they are questioned by Nicodemus, they say to him, "Are you a Galilean, too?" So, we see the hardness of heart, this inability to see, that lack of openness. The blind man in the previous story and in this morning's gospel story are inviting us to be open.

Now, what causes us to be less open? One thing that causes that is ritualism, which is different from ritual. Ritual is something sacred; it ought to move us and change us. When we enter into the ritual, we enter with our very being, with everything, with our minds, our hearts, our emotions. And one ritual we should enter into that way, of course, is Sunday Mass. On the other hand, ritualism gets caught up in things, ritualism gets caught up in actions. Ritualism likes the clothing; it likes the speech. Ritualism likes the incense, ritualism likes the titles, whether it's "Father", "Monsignor", "Your Grace" and so on. We get caught up in all these things, and so, ritualism stifles; it's as if, like arteries, the sight becomes clogged with their own kind of plaque. Today's gospel invites us to be more open, to look around us, to see where we can discover Christ emerging as light to us, so that we may be open to that light by which we see.

One of the many things people are saying, on the negative side, as we are in this state of lockdown, is that God is punishing us. Yet when we read the scriptures, nowhere do we see Jesus delighting in the punishment of others. So, this is a kind of spiritual blindness; it's as if the Holy Spirit wants to lead us, asking us to be open, asking us to learn from what is going on, but many of us don't want to do that. We want to see what we want to see, just like the Pharisees in today's story. It's not that they could not see, they did not want to see. So, is God punishing us? Many people say yes to that. Has God sent COVID to purify us? Many people are saying yes, that is God's way of purifying and punishing us. I don't think that is true at all. I think if we look at it more clearly, we would see a richer answer. When we read the scriptures, we hear Jesus saying in Saint John's Gospel, "I have not come to condemn the world, I have come to save it." And perhaps the most famous passage that people know is John 3:16 – "God so loved the world…" If God so loved the world, how can He take delight in what is happening to us? If God so loves the world, why do we keep saying that God is punishing us? Are we being called to deeper conversion? Yes. Are we being purified by the pandemic? Yes. But we have to draw distinction between that and becoming blind and not open, and ending up saying that God is punishing us.

Pope Francis, my dear friends, said that God is mercy, and he means that both as a noun and as a verb. God is mercy itself, because mercy is what God does; sometimes we don't want to see that and we think people who say so belong to the "rabble" – those who do not know. As we celebrate this morning's gospel and as we continue on our journey, our lives in these difficult times, let us ask Almighty God to really help us see, to be open to new teaching, to new sight and what the pandemic can teach us. Let us remember that we have cast aside certain doctrines; let us not bring them back. Let us remember, as the Mighty Sparrow sang many years ago: *"We have come of age and remember we pass that stage."*

FIFTH WEEK OF LENT

RAISING OF LAZARUS FROM THE DEAD

Sunday March 29, 2020.
Fifth Sunday of Lent.

First Reading: Ezekiel 37: 12-14
Responsorial Psalm: Psalm 130: 1-2, 3-4, 5-6, 7-8
Second Reading: Romans 8: 8-11
Gospel: John 11: 1-45
HOMILY: Archbishop Charles Jason Gordon

Our reading today is another very, very, big text. Huge! Layered with meaning in every direction. Every line, every verse has more symbolic meaning than you could ever believe. What I want to pull out of the text is what I consider its core, its kernel. I want you to hear a line in this text first: "This sickness will not end in death." Say it with me: "This sickness will not end in death."

Now, that is a most remarkable line for us to be reading on this day as we are facing the pandemic throughout the world and here, in Trinidad and Tobago – on the eve of moving into the next stage, as we go into a full lockdown of our country – the panic people are experiencing, all the different ways in which people are now fearful, anxious. Cabin fever has already set in for the children who have been home now a couple weeks, and the parents who have had to be home with them. And, now, we have further restrictions because this sickness seems to be so all-pervasive, so powerful, so invincible; it takes over a country and does what it wants with the country. And yet, we must believe what the word teaches us: "This sickness will not end in death." The sickness will not end in death; that will not be the absolute end!

Now Martha, Mary, Lazarus – they are a family in Bethany that is close to Jesus. Whenever He went to Jerusalem, He would go into the Garden of Gethsemane, up the Mount of Olives and pass along into Bethany. It's a very short distance from Jerusalem, so whenever He's in Jerusalem that's where He stays, with this family. So, He's very close to them and yet, when He got the message, *"Your friend, Lazarus, is ill"*, Jesus does the strangest thing ever: He waits two days. The disciples are confused: *"But I thought He is your good friend."* Jesus' response was, *"Yeah, it is because I love him that I am waiting."* Now, you figure that logic out: *I'm waiting because I love him. I am not rushing to help him because I love him. I am waiting.*

Now, that is a piece of illogic that will boggle your mind for weeks. Because the love of God is displayed in this text in a way that is totally contrary to how we human beings think. We think if God really loves us, He should spare us. If He really loves us, He should not allow things to reach to this stage. If He really loves us, He should have done something to wipe this out already. But Jesus says: *"Because I love him, I'm waiting two days. Because I love him."*

Now, that is a way of understanding that you could only understand if you understand the man born blind. Because, again, in that text it questions who sinned? The man, his mother or his father? Jesus said none of them; the man was born this way that the glory of God may be revealed – as in this case with Lazarus, as in this case with COVID-19. This is happening so that the glory of God will be revealed. How?

Well, look at the text and the emotions in the text. Incredible human emotions! The disciples are confounded: *"How come He's not going back?"* Then there's fear: *"The Jews wanted to stone You the time You were there in Jerusalem, not too long ago! And You're going back?"* Then there's courage: Thomas – whom we call doubting Thomas – comes out and says, *"Let us go to Jerusalem with Him; let's die with Him."* And then, there's grief. When Jesus reaches to Bethany everyone is in deep, deep grief and here, as we see in the shortest line in the whole of scripture, "Jesus wept." Jesus wept, and the people said, *"See, He weeps for His friend. Could He not have treated him as He treated the man born blind? Why couldn't He have cured this one?"* Jesus wept, and He continues to weep. As a human being, He wept for His friend; as Man, He weeps for you and for me. As Man, He feels the whole range of human emotions and He's taken that up into heaven. That's symbolised in the Sacred Heart of Jesus; in every good Catholic home, at one time, as soon as you opened the door of the house, you saw an image of the Sacred Heart of Jesus. It reminds us that God's heart is broken, broken for you and for me because we have not lived all that God has called us to live. The text moves forward again from the desolation and Jesus' weeping, that action of God, and it is in this action of God that something starts to happen, and a range of human emotions change.

If we look again at the faith perspective in this text, the disciples still don't understand who Jesus is. But, then, we meet Martha, who is still, who is at prayer – totally contrary to how we always see her, a busy body of practicalities. Martha is filled with grief and has this incredible dialogue with Jesus when she says: "If You had only been here, my brother would not have died." And Jesus responded, *"But your brother is going to rise again." "I know he will rise again at the resurrection of the dead,"* Martha says. And here, we have the pivotal piece of our story: who is Jesus Christ? Who is He? Jesus says: "Martha, I AM..." He invokes the name by which God revealed Himself to Moses: "I AM the resurrection and the life, he who believes in Me will never die." "I AM the resurrection and the life..." – do you believe this? That Jesus is "the resurrection and the life"? In saying this, Jesus points to something very powerful. The whole community is worried about a man who had died; Jesus is worried about life after the grave. Poor Lazarus, I sympathise with the guy; he dies twice! He dies the first time and Jesus brings him back to life, only for him to die again. Dying once is traumatic enough! Dying twice! But he dies twice, so that the glory of God may be revealed. We hear twice in our text – someone says it on Jesus' entry into Bethany, then Martha repeats it – that Lazarus has been in the grave for four days. In Jewish law, you could not recognise a dead person after four days; they would be too decomposed. And you would never open a tomb after four days; it was against the law, the tradition, the customs, everything. And it is said twice, emphasising the fact that what is going to happen here is going beyond everything. It is not the same as the case of the widow's son who was going on to burial; when Jesus raised him, he was still intact. But after four days, Lazarus is decomposing. Now, what about Mary? Mary is also praying at home; she's the contemplative. She's there in the room, praying quietly, everyone surrounding her, but at a word from Martha, goes out looking for Jesus with whom she also has a dialogue. The line I love most in the text happens when Jesus reaches the tomb and says, *"Roll the stone."* So, there's a divine action, a command. But there must be a human response, because if nobody rolls the stone, then the next action doesn't take place. What is the rolling of the stone? How do we roll the stone? How do we open back the grave? How do we open back that which was death?

You know, we sometimes take great pride in our "graves", eh? All the "graves" where the dead bodies are buried: "My mother hurt me when I was this age – that's why I am this way now." And, "this one did me that – that's how I am this way now." We all have a pile of "graves" that we use as trophies and monuments to explain to other people why we cannot grow up, why we cannot be different, why we cannot be holy and why we cannot become saints. Open the grave! We've made such a monument out of our graves, all the terrible things that were done to us that caused in-credible death for us in our psyche. Let us open the graves that we have made such monuments out of and allow Jesus Christ in.

When the stone in Bethany is rolled, when the grave is open, Jesus simply says: *"Lazarus, come forth. Come out, come out."* In the Book of Ezekiel, our first reading, the prophet says that God means to open the graves of His peo-ple and bring them forth. It is the same language that He uses for the Exodus, for bringing the people out of Egypt into the Promised Land. And it is the same language He's using today, for you and for me, to remind us that this sick-ness will not end in death, but in the revelation of the glory of God.

So, move that stone, move it! Open that grave and, today, as we celebrate Eucharist together, let us hear the words of Jesus Christ: *"Come forth! Come forth!"* Come out of your graves, come out of the death that you've made such a show over. Come out of the death that has been so engaging for us, that we've been hiding behind as an excuse for not becoming holy people. Come out of the death that we've been living in this country: working at manic pace, barely loving each other and barely relating to each other. Come out of the death that we have been creating in this country, where we have taken freedom and moved it to a license and made it into a god. An untouchable freedom that no one can talk to, that impinges on everyone else. Come out of the grave, come out of the grave, because God means to do a renewal in His people, in your life and in my life. But first, we must open the grave; we must recognise it is a grave. We must open it; we must allow Jesus Christ in. The sickness will not end in death, because God is the resurrection and the life.

Jesus is the resurrection and the life and having brought Lazarus forth out of the grave, He says something that is most profound: "Unbind him." Unbind him. Not only must we be raised from the dead, we are to be unbound and it takes the whole community to do this. The action of unbinding restores us. You know how easy it is for a spouse to bind up another spouse? You know exactly which button to press to bind them – do you know what I'm talking about? A friend, a parent, a child knows exactly which button to press to bind the other. Unbind them! Unbind; let them go free.

The very core of our text, what we are working with at the human level, is a range of emotions that are enormous and deep. At the Divine level, what we're working with is a demonstration of God's incredible love for His people, you and me, and a demonstration that death will not have the final say; that death has no more power. Where is your power, O Death? Where is your destruction? Because Jesus Christ has been raised from the dead! This Sunday looks towards Passion Sunday, where we will contemplate the mystery of the Passion of Jesus Christ. We are looking at the Passion, not as the first Jews and the disciples did, we are looking at the Passion with a perspective of the Resurrection, knowing who Jesus Christ is. And as we look at COVID-19, we are looking at it, not as many other people are, we are looking at it from the perspective of who Jesus Christ is. He is the One who, when we roll the stone back, can call us forth from our death. He is the One who calls forth, gives the orders to unbind, to restore the person to right relationship within the community. There is a death worse than what COVID-19 is threatening, and that death is the death we have been living over the last thirty years in our nation – the death of our families, a destruction of integrity, of decency, of fair play, a destruction of living by values and virtues and character and principles. A destruction of trusting people to do the right thing because it is right. A destruction on the level of the family where children have stopped obeying parents, and parents feel powerless in the face of their children. A destruction of our education system where so many children come out of the education system unfit for civilization, with little sense of what is required as a citizen and the responsibility that should be ingrained in us.

There's a death we have been living, as we've seen our murder rate rising constantly. There's a death we have been living as our quality of our life has been diminishing, significantly, over the last thirty years. There is a death we have been living in this country that is more destructive and more pernicious than COVID-19. And Jesus is saying, that death will not end in death but in the glory of God being revealed; He's saying to us: "Come forth from the grave!" We will all see the end of COVID-19, whenever that is. I'm just perturbed that I must wait a little longer for the glory of God to be revealed. But whenever that end comes, we will see the glory of God, but for that, we must move the stone. That means, in your family, you have to move that stone that has stopped communication between you. You have to do the forgiveness work; do it! Don't wait! Do the forgiveness work. You're going to be in the same house; it's going to be really small unless the forgiveness work is done. That's moving the stone. Do the forgiveness work: look in the eyes of your family members, one by one, and say you are sorry, that you didn't understand, you didn't realise – whatever it is, but *ask for forgiveness*. Let us allow these two weeks to be a time of moving the stone – starting that forgiveness work – and allowing Jesus to call us forth from the tomb so that we can be unbinding each other. So that, at the end of this period, rather than death and destruction breaking out, life, joy and resurrection will break forth into our land.

I know many people are itching on these two weeks – panic! Cabin fever before it even starts! This will not end in death, but for it to end in life, we must be engaged and allow Jesus to lead us. Open that grave, open it, that wound that has caused such destruction in your family. And if that person you need to work with is not living with you, call them, Facetime them, WhatsApp them. Engage in forgiveness work in these two weeks, because God will bring life where there seems to be death. Do not wait. And, in that, unbinding will take place and the renewal and rebuilding of our society will take place, and you and I will see the glory of God manifest before us and we will know who God is. Amen.

THE WOMAN CAUGHT IN ADULTERY

Monday March 30, 2020.
Fifth Week of Lent.

First Reading: Daniel 13: 1-9, 15-17, 19-30, 33-62
Responsorial Psalm: Psalm 23: 1-3a, 3b-4, 5, 6
Gospel: John 8: 1-11
HOMILY: Archbishop Charles Jason Gordon

Well, today we have some big, big readings and we are moving closer and closer to this great Mystery, the Mystery of all mysteries: the Mystery of Holy Week and Easter. And, as we move towards it, remember we are in the desert. I think if you didn't remember you're in the desert, today you know! Complete lockdown! Nobody moving, everybody staying at home. And in this desert time, another question is now being proposed: the question of morality, the question of moral choice. If you look at that first reading, you'll see something intriguing: the men had been looking at Susanna for a while. It didn't just happen one day, they were looking at Susanna for a while! And their lust began to grow. And it grew and it grew. And their lust having grown, they then wanted to go from lust to rape, and then from rape to murder. That's the nature of sin sickness: it creeps in like a tiny, tiny seed but when it flowers, it becomes a mighty tree. In our story, we also have the other side of it: the innocent woman who puts her trust in God. Against all odds, against her whole community, against everyone condemning her, she puts her trust in God and is unshaken in her trust. She becomes a type for Jesus; they become a type for the crowd, the Pharisees and the whole institution of Israel that will condemn Jesus. And so, we now have played out before us the extensive drama that will unfold in Holy Week. The innocent woman and sin that is entered into, over and over, until it flowers, grows, becomes a mighty tree and takes over the whole. Where are we in that drama? I know, I know – we belong to the side of the innocent one, not so? Correct? Hmm, I wish! How has sin crept into your life? As a little seed? How have you allowed it to grow? How has that growth of sin become mature and how is it evolving into something else? That's what the story is about.

On another level, the story is about concupiscence. Concupiscence is the inclination to sin that came through Adam and Eve in the Fall, and it's three-fold. We first encountered it on the First Sunday in Lent as a triple concupiscence reflected in the three temptations Christ had to face – lust of the flesh, which is what we're dealing with here; lust of the eyes, which is all the glory and fanciness that the world offers that we lust for; and pride of life, which is the original sin where we believe that we are better than God. This triple concupiscence which we met at the beginning of Lent, comes back to us at this moment, as we're preparing to face Holy Week celebrations in one week's time – the central Mystery of our faith. Because it is in this triple concupiscence that we understand our desperate need for a Saviour, and thank God we know His name! His name is Jesus Christ. The voice of the young one who speaks out in prophecy to save Susana is a voice of incredible reason and wisdom. The old people had become dumb and the young man had wisdom – isn't that a wonderful contrast? We now have a whole movement happening in our text; because of his intervention she is seen to be the innocent one and the two lecherous men are condemned.

Now, we have the flip text in our gospel where the old men have brought a woman caught in the very act of committing adultery but, again, in this text there is no man. Where's the man? She was committing adultery by herself, clearly! So, there's a lot of humour happening in the text but, for our purposes, there's one point here: they are condemning in order to trap Jesus. So, we are back to the first reading; this is not a straight conversation, this is a trap, a testing.

Jesus bends down and writes in the sand, and they keep insisting. He writes in the sand again and then they leave – one by one. And the question the text asks of us is this: Who writes with His finger? And who writes twice? What is being read here is Jesus becoming a type for God. Up on Mount Sinai, God used His finger to write the Law and He wrote it twice, because the first time Moses broke the tablets because of the disobedience of the people. Here we have the whole coming together of salvation history, of our rebellion and God's mercy, of our licentiousness and God's incredible mercy. This text reflects mercy, extreme mercy, *really* extreme mercy to this woman! And what this text speaks to you and to me, as we're preparing ourselves for the big sacred mysteries in two weeks' time, is that if we have the eyes to see, we will know that we need a Saviour. And if we have our heart wide open, we will know that this Saviour is a God of mercy, a God of incredible, incredible mercy.

Today, as we come to the readings, let us see the way in which concupiscence has taken hold in our life, the ways in which we have given in to lust of the flesh, lust of the eyes and pride of life. But let us also see the incredible mercy

96

that God has for this woman, that Jesus writes a new law, and it is a law of mercy. And in that, the woman finds her freedom but is given the command: "Go and sin no more." So, let us turn to the loving gaze of God, who alone can cure us of concupiscence and all of our sin-sickness and beg as Susana did, plead as this woman did, for the mercy of our God. Amen.

The Father Is Always with the Son

Tuesday March 31, 2020.
Fifth Week of Lent.

First Reading: Numbers 21: 4-9
Responsorial Psalm: Psalm 102: 2-3, 16-18, 19-21
Gospel: John 8: 21-30
HOMILY: Archbishop Charles Jason Gordon

So, today again we are in the desert, remember. And this is the desert of deserts, because this is not just curtailing activity; we are now locked down! We are in this very confined space, wherever we are – we are in the desert. And if we remember that we're in the desert, then we remember that there are things that we must undergo here. So, the Israelites at Mount Hor, on the road they were quarrelling against God and quarrelling against Moses. Why were they quarrelling? You see, they were hungry. God had given them manna to eat in the desert but, after a while, they grew dissatisfied with the manna. Who could continue eating "this unsatisfying food?"

Now, you know many people say that about the Eucharist. And now, look at us! In the desert, fasting even from the Eucharist! In the desert, as they complained against God and against Moses, fiery serpents came and started to destroy and devour the people. That sound like our kind of situation today, eh? Because we have become the most ungrateful people the world has ever known! We've had more than any generation before us: more excess wealth, more gadgets, more technology, more of everything! There was a documentary that talked about the 19th century house – you know, we glamorise the good old days – but by the time that poor woman was finished cooking, cleaning and washing, she had no strength left for anything else in in her day. All the gadgets we have make life a lot easier today than it used to be a hundred and fifty years ago, and yet, we are dissatisfied with our life, dissatisfied with so many things and we always believe that there is more that we should have. And now that this fiery serpent called COVID-19 has come and is biting us – and it's biting us hard – it is making us recognise things and we now have a choice to make. God said to Moses, "Fashion a bronze serpent and put it on a standard, and if anyone is bitten by a serpent and looks on it, he will live." What is God doing? He's turning that instrument of death into an instrument of life; the thing that brought horror, terror to the people of Israel. Remember that snakes were used in the plagues in Egypt to help Pharaoh to understand he had to listen. The plagues of snakes that are coming is a terrifying kind of plague and, yet, that same terror, that same horror turned, lifted up, becomes a symbol of life and the source of healing.

Up to today, the medical profession uses the bronze standard with the serpent on it as a sign of healing and as a sign of life that the medical profession is sworn to. So how do we lift up this microbe? How do we lift it up and put it on a bronze standard so that it becomes a symbol of life for us? How do we lift it up? That's the question that is facing you and me today, as we are in this desert heading towards the greatest celebration that the Church has to offer. As we are heading towards this great celebration, this Triduum, this microbe is biting at us. And if it is biting at us, we can either give way to its bite and yield to death, or lift it up and yield to life.

In the gospel, they don't understand who Jesus is, even though twice He says, "I am He", the second time saying: *"When you lift up the Son of Man, when you lift Him up, then you will know that I am He."* He invokes the "I AM", which is the name by which God revealed Himself to Moses, and Jesus would be revealed when He is lifted up. There's something about suffering, about "lifting up" for the revelation of God. When the people in the desert looked upon the bronze standard with the serpent, they looked *up* towards God and they were healed. When they looked *down* at the serpents on the ground, they were terrified. And, today, you have a choice: you could look up towards God and receive the healing that you need to live in this time, or you could look down towards the microbe and be filled with horror, fear, terror, all kinds of internal strife.

The invitation of our readings today is to *lift it up*. Lift it up! How do we lift it up? Well, let's not only see the death that COVID-19 has brought us, let's also see the opportunity of being in our houses today – the opportunity of being a family, of being together, opportunity of being able to pray together. Create a space, a little chapel, in your home where your family can come together once, twice or three times a day for short periods of prayer. A space where you can go, where the children can go, where you can kneel and lift up this time that we are living – lift it up to Him.

As we lift it up to God in prayer, we'll start to see as God sees, no longer looking at COVID-19 through fear. We'll begin to see as God sees because we are becoming His people, and the whole world now knows that we are not in charge, our science cannot save us, that we are in need of a Saviour and His name is Jesus Christ. That He was lifted up for all to see and the glory of God is Jesus Christ on the Cross and that God, Himself, suffered and died that you and I may have life.

IF THE SON OF MAN MAKES YOU FREE, YOU WILL BE FREE, INDEED

Wednesday April 1, 2020.
Fifth Week of Lent.

First Reading: Daniel 3: 14-20, 91-92, 95
Responsorial Psalm: Daniel 3: 52-56
Gospel: John 8: 31-42
HOMILY: Archbishop Charles Jason Gordon

What is the nature of faith? What is the nature of faith? That's what we're looking at today. Before Shadrach, Meshach and Abednego were challenged by the king to bow to him at the time of offering, sacrifice and prayer, do you think they thought they could have done it? Do you think they would have sat back and said, *"Oh! Oh, I'm ready to die! I'm ready to do this, I'm ready!"* No, before they were challenged, they simply lived as they were living and hoped that God would give them the courage to do what they needed to do. At the moment at which they were challenged, something happened and they got a grace, a singular grace, to put God first before any other god, a grace to witness to the truth, regardless of the consequence of that witness. And that grace is what we're working with in our first reading today. They could easily have done like everybody else in Jerusalem because the king, Nebuchadnezzar, was forcing every land, every realm, every people to bow to him as God and to do away with their culture, to do away with their gods. Why? Because if he united them in the belief that he was God, he would have a united realm, a people that was one. But Israel was not bowing and incurred his wrath. Here we now have these three young men; did they believe they could? They received the grace and they did.

Before COVID-19, did you believe that you could stay in your house, not go out, not have any extra activities, not live the manic life you were living two weeks ago, not have the engagements that consumed all your time? Did you believe you could do that? No. Now, we have an opportunity for something else and this, too, is a question of faith. Because, you know, we could be plunged into the desert and still make up manic activity inside the desert to distract us from what the purpose of the desert is – which is giving our hearts to God. We could make up activities easily, we can find all kinds of foolish things to do instead of using this time in devotion to God.

Shadrach, Meshach and Abednego plunged into the challenge: say yes, and put God first! They are thrown into the fire. Do you think it's going to be easy? It's not going to be easy; we're going to be thrown into the fire. Some of you are feeling the fire on your feet already, the fire of cabin fever! You know that fire; you feeling it already and it doh feel nice! Well, they walked in the fire and the king realised it wasn't just them walking; there was one like a Son of God walking with them and they were unbound. You may feel bound, you may feel tied up, but if you walk this fire with faith, you will be unbound and there will be One walking with you who is like a Son of God. This time would be a time of incredible intimacy and closeness with God, this time during which we're tested by the fire of faith. You would have been purified, and purer yet than gold seven times refined. These three allowed themselves to put God first. Are you allowing yourself to put God first in this fire that you are in? Put Him first and walk this fire with Him.

Our gospel reading is another story of faith. In the gospel, Jesus is saying to the Jews, "If you make My word your home, you will indeed be My disciples; and you will learn the truth and the truth will set you free." That's what we do in the fire. *Make His word our home.* Now, you have a set of time you do not know what to do with, a pile of time you never expected to have! Previously, you were too busy to pray, too busy to read the scriptures, too busy for devotion, too busy for all these things; you have time now. Make His word your home. What does that mean? Well, one way of doing it is tuning into Mass every day and following the readings. Take the readings before you come to Mass or afterwards, sit with them and ponder them so that the word of God becomes like a home to you. So that you start living in the word and allowing the word to live in you: *"If you make My word your home you will be My disciples and you will be set free."* There's a wonderful text here that says so: *"If the Son makes you free, you're free indeed"*, and that's what true freedom is.

We thought that true freedom is doing what you want, when you want, how you want, as you like it. That's not true freedom, that's enslavement to somebody else and some other set of ideals. Real freedom is when we make the Word of God our home; when that Word is our home and we live in Him and He lives in us, and we do as He asks and allow Him to lead us to the truth. Because when we come to true freedom, our will and His will are so aligned that we find we are doing what love requires, because the will of God is always love. The will of God is always love, and that's why

He said to them, *"If Abraham were your father you would do as Abraham did; he put his faith in God and you would put your faith in Me."* To be a person of faith is to allow God to take you through that fire, to transform your life so that your will and His will become so aligned that there's no space between His will and your will. And there, you will find freedom, the only true freedom that would make sense to anybody and the only true freedom that would allow your life to flourish. Then, walking in the fire of cabin fever, walking in the fire of COVID-19, walking in the fire of desolation, of challenge there will be another One walking with you, because you have made His word your home and you will live in Him and He will live in you. That's the promise of Jesus Christ: this nuptial union, this intimacy with God that every single one of us is called to today, today, today!

Look at what you've done for the last two or the first two days of lockdown. How did you spend the time? How have you used it? Have you used it as if it were a curse, or have you used it as a blessing and an invitation? You didn't ask for it, you're thrown into it. Now, through faith, see this as the best of times; through faith, use this time to draw close to Him. Amen.

"BEFORE ABRAHAM EVER WAS, I AM."

Thursday April 2, 2020.
Fifth Week of Lent.

First Reading: Genesis 17: 3-9
Responsorial Psalm: Psalm 105: 4-5, 6-7, 8-9
Gospel: John 8: 51-59
HOMILY Archbishop Charles Jason Gordon

So, this is the great week where we have the big, big stories of faith! We've seen Susanna and that drama around morality and what happens when lust gets out of hand. We've seen Shadrach, Meshach and Abednego walking through the fire. Now, we have a drama that is bigger than everything else we've seen. We are taken back to Abraham and, remember, Abraham is the father of faith. Abraham is the one with whom God makes a covenant, and in that covenant Abraham will be a blessing to a multitude of nations. As we hear in our text, Abraham bowed to the ground and God said to him, "Here now is My Covenant with you..." *"Here now is My Covenant with you"*! A covenant is a *binding relationship* between two parties. In the Old Testament they didn't have lawyers, so you didn't go "lawyer up" and make a bullet-proof agreement and have it signed. You made a covenant, and the covenant would be: you will do this and I will do that, and we agree to it. There are many ways to seal a covenant. We see here, with Abraham, the way of sealing the covenant is through a blood sacrifice. Abraham prepared the animals and God sent fire on the animals and burnt them up as a holocaust, so that those animals can never be eaten or had or seen again.

Because the covenant is irrevocable, the very source of the covenant – the blood and the animal – is completely given over and can never be taken back.

Now, God first made a covenant with Adam; we know what happened to that one, they broke that one properly! His second covenant was with Noah: God said He will never mash up the world by water and flood again, but the people must behave well. Well, they broke that one, too. Now He makes a covenant with Abraham, and the covenant with Abraham has several pieces to it. It's so important that the Bible records it three different times. First, he must leave his land and his people and go to a new land and a new people – a foreshadowing of the Exodus. Second, his name was changed and, to name somebody is to be father to that person. By changing his name, God is saying: *"I become your Father this day and I give you a new name: you're no longer Abram, you're now Abraham."* Third, is a covenant that is signed by circumcision; maybe God was saying, *"You know, they didn't get the point of it the last time but, maybe if We hurt them where it really hurts, maybe they might get the point this time and remember."* Well, we know what happened to that one; they forgot that, too. But this Covenant with Abraham is a covenant that is made for all generations; Abraham will become a blessing to a multitude of nations. Abraham will take God as his God, and God, on His part, will protect Abraham and His people. The covenant with Adam and Eve was made with a couple, with Noah a family; with Abraham, it is with a multitude of nations.

Let us move to the gospel reading now, to Jesus and the Jews in their dialogue. Jesus is making some very important points; He says to them, "Truly I say to you, whoever keeps

My word will never die." And they respond: *"Well, Abraham is dead, the prophets are dead – who are You? Who are You claiming to be?"* And each time they push *Him, He raises the bar: "If I was seeking My own glory that would be no glory at all. My glory is conferred by the Father."* In John's Gospel, the glory of God is seen at the moment of the crucifixion, revealed when Jesus gives everything He has in complete love, because we now see the full extent of God's love and what love really, really looks like. But in this Covenant, this new dispensation, Jesus is saying: "I tell you solemnly, before Abraham ever was, I AM." "I AM" is the name that God revealed to Moses in the burning bush in the desert: "I AM who I AM." In other words, Jesus might as well have said to them: *"Don't worry about Abraham; I AM the one who appeared to Moses in the burning bush, because I AM God."*

Now, I want you to feel the full shock and horror of this! The last time a man told me he was God, I took him to St. Ann's and they locked him up there for about three or four months; he was having a psychotic episode. Now, the Jews pick up stones to stone Jesus. You must understand and hear that, because it means they understand what He is saying: that He is claiming to be God, and that's a sin of blasphemy. It was against the Law and that is why they prepare to stone Him. They were invoking the law that anyone who blasphemes should be put to death because Jesus is claiming to be God. And, here, in His claim to be God, we now have very little wriggle room in what we do with Jesus. Because if He is not God, lock Him up in St. Ann's! If He is God, then what do we do with Him? If He is not God, then He must be a liar or a madman. But, if He is, what do we do with Him? And this is the drama that is put before you today. Who do you say He is? When Jesus says, "Before Abraham ever was, I AM", invoking the identity of God and saying that the glory of God will be revealed, this plays forward to the Last Supper and to the Cross where He makes a final covenant, a covenant in blood, the covenant of the sacrifice of a Lamb. That's what we celebrate every time we come to this altar: that the covenant is no longer a covenant for which Abraham paid the price of circumcision. This covenant is a covenant where God has paid the supreme price by giving us His Son, Jesus Christ, who gave His blood and His body for our salvation. The Covenant of Jesus Christ is called the last and eternal covenant; it is the supreme offering of God, because what we have here is the supreme image of love.

Love is easy when the beloved is loving you back, not so? When the beloved is giving you thunder, what do you do? When the beloved is hitting back, is rejecting, is angry at you, belittling you? When that is the case and you keep loving, that's a higher form of love. Remember love is not a feeling, eh? Is not the pitter-patter of your heart when a beloved walks in the door! Love is a verb, an action word! We've learned, since we were "this high", that a verb is something you *do*, not something you feel. This is a supreme symbol of what love really looks like, because this cross is how love has been displayed. We took everything negative, every vile emotion that the human could ever muster in their heart and soul, and we threw it on to Jesus on the cross. And what did He do? He loved in return: "Father, forgive them, they know not what they do." Not only did He give love in return, in the rush He "beg-off" for us, too! That's the highest form of love that we will ever see. If this is the covenant by which we have become children of God, this is what we've been called to imitate. Now, you and I have a serious problem, because if that's the high standard of the covenant, what's the standard of your loving? What's the quality of your loving? What's the quality of your forgiveness? What's the quality of your giving to those who are not loving you back? That is the drama of our text today, because as we're moving closer to the Passion, we're moving deeper into the heart and soul of the Mystery of faith that we are celebrating.

Today, reflect on the quality of your loving, because God has loved us with everything He has. We can't afford conditional love: "I love you if you behave good", "I will love you if you love me back", "I will love you if you do the things I like", "I will love you if you act the way I want you to act" – that's not love! Love, in its highest form, is expressed in this incredible symbol of the cross. That symbol is what we must ponder on this day, because this is what God did so we could become children of God.

JESUS ELUDES ARREST

Friday April 3, 2020.
Fifth Week of Lent.

First Reading: Jeremiah 20: 10-13
Responsorial Psalm: Psalm 18: 2-3a, 3bc-4, 5-6, 7
Gospel: John 10: 31-42
HOMILY: Archbishop Charles Jason Gordon

As we come to this Friday before the drama begins – because Sunday is Palm Sunday and we enter into the holiest of all weeks – the Church is reminding us now, in very clear terms, why they crucified Jesus Christ. And to help us understand, they've taken us back to a type before Jesus – Jeremiah, who experienced exactly what Jesus experienced. His enemies were all round: "Terror on every side!" he says. They decried and disparaged him: "Let us denounce him!" And all who used to be his friends now watch for his downfall. Why? Jeremiah was asked to speak a word from God in a very difficult time, at a time when the people had turned their hearts away from God. And because they turned their hearts away from God, they couldn't hear the word of God. Because they had made their freedoms more important than their obedience to God, they could not hear the word of God. Because they made their lifestyle more important than the word of God, they could not hear the word of God. Because they wanted to do what they wanted to do – as very strong-willed people who had no care for the poor or for those on the margins of society – they could not hear the word of God. Because they persisted in their rebellion against God,

God sent them prophets, and still, they could not hear the word of God.

Now, I'm only talking about Jerusalem back in the day, eh! Don't pick up stones and start looking for me now! Is Jerusalem back in the day I talking about; let us get that really clear! When we hear why they wanted to stone Jeremiah, if that stone fall in your garden, you know what to do! You see, we are living in a time like the time of Jeremiah where the heart of the people has turned away from God, where the heart of the people has become so coarse and so hard that even to hear what God has to say is so difficult. We are in times much like the times of Jeremiah, because in our day, people want to do what they want to do, regardless of what the word of God says and regardless of what God Himself says, because we don't put any stock in God, in the word of God or in the Church. We are smart and bright people and we know for ourselves what is right and what is wrong and what we choose, we know it is right. Truth has no sway in our world any more, none at all! It has nothing to do with what is true; is how I feel, what I like, what I want!

And then, on Friday March 13th we were plunged into the desert of COVID, and all of a sudden, our eyes are opening and we're realising we're not as powerful as we thought we were. We're certainly not as invincible as we thought we were; we're not in control in the way we thought we were and we certainly did not get it right! And that's the purpose of the desert: to open the eyes of the blind. Let us be clear on this one, okay? The real blind people, you and me, we are the blind ones because we thought we knew and we thought we could see. Being plunged into this desert of

COVID-19, we are recognising a lot of what we thought was vision was really half-sightedness and blindness. And because we're recognising that, we're also realising that God is here in the midst of this terrible thing; a terrible thing, but an incredible opportunity that we have.

So, let's go to the gospel reading now from this perspective, and see what the gospel is saying. They were picking up stones to stone Jesus; why? This is taking up from the events of yesterday's gospel; they wanted to stone Him because He had said, "Before Abraham ever was, I AM." He invoked the name of God, the "I AM Who AM"; He invoked the name of God, claiming to be God. So, let's get that one clear: He's claiming to be God and, as I said yesterday, if Jesus claims to be God, He leaves us no wriggle room. It isn't that somebody, after the fact, decided, "Oh, maybe He was God," and made Him into God; *He* is claiming to be God! "Before Abraham ever was, I AM". And, because He's claiming to be God, they want to stone Him.

Now, we are here at the Feast of the Dedication and this is the second-to-last great festival that Jesus turned upside down. The first is the Sabbath, because no one is allowed to work on the Sabbath, but Jesus works on the Sabbath! Why? Because He is *God* – God alone is permitted to work on the Sabbath. Jesus said the Sabbath is made for man, not man for the Sabbath; He turns the Sabbath inside out. Then, at the Feast of Tabernacles where they celebrate the water that gushed forth from the desert, Jesus turns Himself into the living water. On the last and greatest day of the festival, He cried out in a loud voice: *"Let anyone who thirsts, let that one come to Me because from his soul will flow fountains of living water."* He turns Himself into the living water.

In the last feast, which is the Feast of the Passover – and we recall that next week on Holy Thursday when we celebrate the Last Supper – He makes Himself into the spotless lamb that is sacrificed for our sake, thus becoming the Lamb of God whose blood, sprinkled on the doorposts, removes all of our sin. Now, in this Feast of the Dedication, what they're celebrating is the dedication of the temple – this grand beautiful building, magnificent to the eye. The temple was consecrated as a place of God. You know what He says here? *"You're disparaging One that God has consecrated and sent into the world."* He's comparing *Himself*, consecrated by God, with the *temple* that was consecrated by the high priests. He has undone the Feast of the Dedication by making Himself into the Consecrated One and showing that everything, every feast of Israel, is pointing to Him because He has come as the One to save mankind.

We find ourselves in a wonderful place on this Fifth Friday of Lent. Fridays are days of repentance. Jesus is the Consecrated One, the Living Water, Master of the Sabbath, the great "I AM" – that's who He is. Who are you? Who are you, and who do you think you are in relationship to Him? I want us to really spend some time today and ponder the ways in which we have lived in rebellion to God – ponder the ways that we have resisted bending our heart to His will, ponder the ways in which our sin-sickness has blinded us to the truth that we are merely fragile vessels, earthenware vessels containing such a great treasure, so that everyone will know that the treasure is *Him*, not us.

Ponder the areas in your life where you make choices against God; ponder the areas in your life where He has been calling you to repentance but you have not heard. Ponder,

ponder deeply, the rebelliousness in your own heart that turns your heart away from God to do what you want to do; the rebelliousness that creates anger whenever you are challenged in a particular area, creates defensiveness, creates a stone wall. Ponder! I beg you, ponder! Because if we ponder together the ways in which we have been rebellious to God, we will find the grace in this day and through this Eucharist, this encounter with Christ, to turn our hearts back to God! This would be a wonderful moment, an incredible opportunity of grace and a marvellous time in which we live. I invite you, I invite you today: *"If today you hear His voice, harden not your hearts as on that day at Meribah in the desert, when your fathers put Me to the test."* If you hear His voice today, open wide your hearts and beg mercy and grace of the Holy Spirit to lead you into the very heart of our God.

Let us pray: Father, we thank You for Your incredible love for us. You love us even when we don't deserve it. When we turn our hearts fully or halfway against You, You still pour Your incredible love out on us relentlessly, O God. Today, O Lord, we recognise that we have sinned, we have done what is wrong. We've trampled on Your word and we we've trampled on other people. We've trampled on the poor, we've trampled on what is sacred. O God, we've not even kept the Sabbath, the holy days, sacred and we've not kept our time of dedication to You sacred. We have sinned, Lord, in so many ways. We have sinned and we come to You, beseeching You this day, have mercy on Your people, O God! Have mercy because we have sinned against You. We ask You, Lord, to show Your mercy, not only to us who participate in this Eucharist, but to our whole world, Lord. And, through us, reach to the world so that Your mercy, Lord, and Your compassion may be visited on all Your people. *Lord, hear us.*

We pray, Lord, for Your Church in these days, that She may be a beacon of hope and light, bringing broken humanity to encounter Your love. *Lord, hear us.*

We pray, Lord, Your mercy on the Holy Father, that You will give him courage and guide him, O God, in these days, that he may be that voice, that clarion voice, that calls broken humanity to You. *Lord hear us.*

We pray, Lord, for our nation, Trinidad and Tobago, that You may bless us, Lord, and give us grace and courage for what we do in these days. *Lord hear us.*

We pray, Lord, for those who participate from all nations, that You would bless them and their leaders. We pray for Barbados, for St. Vincent and the Grenadines, for St. Lucia. We pray for Canada and America and all the many places from which people have sent in requests and said that they are with us. *Lord hear us.*

For the many intentions that we have received and placed in our prayer basket, that You may hear and know, understand and bless. *Lord hear us.*

We bring our prayer to the Father through Christ Jesus our Lord.

O God, Who by the grace of Your Holy Spirit, tem-pered the soul of Gordon Anthony Pantin with forti-tude and humility, and raised him to be priest and Archbishop of the Archdiocese of Port of Spain so that he may be bearer of Your life-giving word to the peo-ple of Trinidad and Tobago, grant us grace to be strong in faith, humbly confident in Your aid and tire-less in doing good. Bestow upon us, we humbly pray, through the intercession of this beloved servant of yours, Gordon Anthony Pantin, the special grace which we seek from Your sovereign goodness in the name of Jesus Christ, our Lord. Amen.

BETTER FOR ONE MAN TO DIE FOR THE PEOPLE

Saturday April 4, 2020.
Fifth Week of Lent.

First Reading: Ezekiel 37: 21-28
Responsorial Psalm: Jeremiah 31: 10, 11-12abcd, 13
Gospel: John 11: 45-56
HOMILY: Archbishop Charles Jason Gordon

We are getting much closer to the action, much closer to the drama, closer to this Holy Week time where everything starts coming together. This week that we are entering is the holiest of all weeks and, in this holiest of weeks, we have to remember that it is for a reason that Jesus gives Himself over. We see in the prophet Ezekiel, a prophecy of the gathering of the lost tribes of Israel and the prophet says four things that we must remember. He says God will send One who will *gather* the scattered tribes into one, will *cleanse* them, will be with them and *lead them as David* their King, and that this would be a *covenant* that lasts forever. The gathering, the cleansing, David, a perpetual covenant – what is the prophet speaking about and how has that prophecy been realised? That's what our gospel is speaking to us today.

In the gospel, we have the high priest, Caiaphas saying: *"It is better that one man die than the whole nation perish."* One man dies for the sake of the whole nation and that one man, we know His name: Jesus Christ; He dies that we can live. He gathers the lost tribes into one, He washes them – and how does He wash them? He washes them with the blood and water that flow from His side, but He also washes

118

them in baptism to bring them into the family of God, to make them – and us – part of the family of God. He is a descendant of David, a King like David, and this is a covenant that lasts forever, as we will hear later in the Mass. When we raise the chalice for the Consecration, we say: "This is the chalice of My Blood, the Blood of the new and eternal covenant…" – new and eternal. New; if it is new it means there was an old covenant that has been superseded. Eternal means that there will be no covenant to come after this. Therefore, this covenant is both new and eternal.

What we have in our readings today is the coming together of the narrative, the bringing together of the drama of the new covenant that Jesus will enact on Holy Thursday and on Good Friday, this new covenant of giving Himself to us in bread and in wine, then by giving Himself to us on the cross. This new covenant, which will be enacted in this week that is coming, shows that one man will die so that all the people can live – and you are part of all that people. You know, many times we have no thought of what Jesus did; why He died or the purpose of His life. I'm asking you to contemplate that today. That this one man died that we could be gathered into the one family of God. The new Israel is a Church and that's why Jesus had twelve apostles – the twelve apostles are for the twelve tribes of Israel. Each one sits in one of the tribes and gathers them into unity, and that's why the unity of the apostles around Jesus is so important. And, after the death of Jesus, why the unity of the bishops around the Pope is so important, and why the unity of the priests around the bishops is so important, and why the unity of the faithful around the priests is so important.

Because it is that gathering into unity that Jesus came to accomplish, and this unity is sacramental for us in the Church.

One of the things we, as Trinidadians, don't know how to do well, is unity. We love, we love to have our own way! We love to create this division, we love to create disunity! But the purpose of Jesus, in giving Himself, is to gather into unity all the people of God. How have you done with unity? How have you done? Have you been a person of unity, a person who really has sought, and worked hard for, the uniting of people in one mind, one heart, one action? Or have you been the kind of person that will always put the spoke in the wheel and always make it difficult for the unity to happen? Bad talk, gossip, do this, do that, so that we have constant disunity? Disunity is a tool of the devil! It is!

Unity doesn't mean uniformity and it doesn't mean we all have to be like cookie-cutters, looking the same way. It doesn't mean that we have to look alike, talk alike, think alike – no, no, no! God created us as individuals! But He's given us free will and we could use that free will to shatter the unity and create division and disunity, or we can use our free will to *choose* to be in unity, to *choose* to pull together, to *choose* to see that we are the body of Christ. The hand cannot say to the foot: "I don't like you", and the head cannot say to the arm, "Get away from me!" The body, if it does not work as one, is sick, and there is a sickness in the body of Christ and that sickness is disunity. How do we come to healthy unity, where it is not that everybody is either a doormat or doing what they want to do, when they want to do it? It is about all of us, all of us, every single one of us seeking the will of God and putting our hearts to seeking God's will. And making God's will above everything else, and praying and discerning until we come to that will of God.

Working towards coming to and living that will is a sign of the kingdom of God here on earth. And it's a sign of the kingdom that is very difficult for us as human beings, generally. But is a real difficult one for us as Trinidadians and Tobagonians – it is! That sign of unity is so difficult for us as Caribbean people, so difficult for us as Barbadians and Vincentians and St Lucians. So difficult for us because we like to have our own way, our own say and to shine in the sun! Our readings today tell us that Jesus is the new David, He is the one that gathers the lost tribes, He is the one that washes us and He has given us a covenant for eternity. The prophecy of Ezekiel has been fulfilled, but the only way it is not fulfilled is when we choose disunity as opposed to unity.

HOLY WEEK

PALM SUNDAY OF THE PASSION OF THE LORD

THE CENTURION'S CONFESSION

5 April 2020 – Year A.

First Reading: Isaiah 50: 4-7
Responsorial Psalm: Psalm 22: 8-9, 17-18, 19-20, 23-24
Second Reading: Philippians 2:6-11
Gospel: Matthew 26: 14 – 27: 66
HOMILY: Archbishop Charles Jason Gordon

I do not know if you want the good news or the bad news first! Whichever one it is: we will be reading this entire Passion again on Good Friday. It is coming! But, on Good Friday, we will read the whole thing again from the other perspective: the perspective of John's Gospel.

And why do we read the Passion? Because this week is The Most Holy Week in the Church's entire year! So this reading – sandwiched between Palm Sunday on the one hand and Good Friday on the other – facilitates our understanding of this event, the most sacred event that has ever happened in human history.

Many, many years ago, as parish priest in the Gonzales community, I went to the home of one of the gang leaders I knew; it was a Friday evening. As I got there, his wife said to me; "You are the right man to come, yes! You are the right man! Glad you come now! Come, come, come, come!" And she took me inside to where this gang leader was sitting down on the ground sobbing, just sobbing. He was watching *"The Passion of the Christ"* movie, and this just left him undone inside. So, I sat on the ground with him and said nothing for what seemed like forever, until he turned to me and said, "Father, I can't believe this man do all this for we! He do all this for we? Sinful we? He do all this for we?" And that is the heart of the Mystery which we celebrate in this week that is most holy in all the world.

Many times, we go through Holy Week and we look at the events and experiences of Jesus from one perspective: that of a man who had all this physical suffering. This year, I want you to look at it from another perspective. The perspective of our Second Reading: *"Though His state was divine, He did not cling to His equality with God but emptied himself, becoming human, and being as all men are, He was humbler yet unto obedience and death on the cross."* See what we contemplate in this mystery of suffering that God has endured for your sake and for mine? He does all this for we! He has endured this for you, for me, for our sins and for our salvation. But see, also, from this perspective, as we listen to the text, that He "emptied Himself" and became "even humbler" by taking on the form of a slave. Consider this: in the Roman law, a Roman who was put to death would be given a dignified death; he would be beheaded. But a slave was given the most scandalous, torturous death, the form that was the most shameful and humiliating – and that was the cross. That is what I want us to meditate upon as we enter into this year's Holy Week. That God has taken on the form of a slave and taken on Himself a most humiliating death!

Have you ever been publicly humiliated? Does it feel different from physical suffering? Does it feel more, or less, than physical suffering? To be publicly humiliated is really one of the worst forms of suffering. Because it is not just in your body, but in every part of your being, everywhere in you! What we are dealing with, from this perspective of the Second Reading, is God enduring the most physical suffering and public humiliation there ever was. And I want you to hold this together because this is a mystery bigger than my mind can hold.

We see Jesus is in the garden, praying. Scripture says He is sweating blood and tears. So, this is not a walk in the park and a, *"Come, bring it on! Give Me the cross let Me run up Jerusalem!"* This is sweating blood and tears! This is Him agonising. This is Him at the edge of His humanity; God agonising for you and for me! Remember in the garden, Adam said no, rebelled and walked away from God. In this garden, Jesus, the new Adam, says yes and walks towards God, towards displaying the glory of God, which is the cross. And we have to see in this mystery of the Garden of Gethsemane: Paradise. That is why Jesus will say on the cross: "Today you will be with Me in Paradise". Jesus opened back Paradise! Remember Paradise was closed, with angels guarding against anyone entering. He opens it back, and how does He do it? Through obedience unto death. Obedience unto death.

You know, we do not understand the nature of obedience. We think that obedience is servitude and so we rebel against the notion of obedience itself. Yet, obedience is at the very core and centre of the spiritual life. We cannot be disciples without obedience to God. Does it come easily? No, it doesn't! Jesus is sweating blood and tears! He is sweating blood and tears as He yields His whole human faculty to God and goes to the cross. And, in this, He undoes the sin of Adam and the rebellion against God and opens up a pathway for us towards God, to this God who invites us all to surrender our will to His will. That is what Jesus does: "Take this cup away from Me. Yet, not My will, O God, but Your will be done".

"Take this cup away from Me." Are we today stopping at this sentence as we face the COVID virus? Are we saying only, "Lord take this away from us, take this away from us?" But we must go to the next sentence, we have to go to that next sentence: "Not my will, but Your will be done". We have to reach to that next sentence because it is only in that place we will start to understand the truth of the mystery of salvation and understand the truth of discipleship. Only in that sentence will we understand who we are, and understand what God has done in and through Jesus Christ for each of us. So, we can see that my boy was right: "Father, I can't believe this man do all this for us." All this? Sinful us? All this suffering?

This mystery is so big. It is so huge. I want you to take up this piece from the garden: bending your will to God's will – I want you to hold on to that for the entire Holy Week. Are you bending yourself to the will of God? Or are you seeking to bend God's will to your own? What are you doing? As you journey through this holiest of all weeks ask yourself, every single day, if you are bending to His will. Is

126

your will being bent towards the will of God, or are you holding on to your willfulness and doing what you want? During this week, let this piece from the garden move us towards becoming a humbler people. Imitate this Second Reading and empty yourself; we call this self-emptying, *"kenosis"*. Let us empty ourselves of what we want, what we think, what we like or what we would do. And let us come as Jesus did in that garden, kneeling before His Father with sweat and tears. Let us say with Him: "Father, Father, take this cup away from us. Take this COVID-19 away from us, take this suffering and death away from us, take this self-isolation away from us. Take this boredom away from us, take this drudgery, take it away from us; take this terrible confinement away from us!" But do not stop there! Please, I beg you, do not stop there; continue to the next sentence. Follow Jesus all the way in His Passion and say with Him: "Not my will, O God, but Your will be done." And let us, in this holiest of all weeks, surrender our life to Jesus Christ, to the grace of God our Father. And let us come out of this week emptying – really, really emptying – consciously giving up our willfulness and giving in to God, who alone has the plan of life and who alone can bring life where there seems only to be death. Amen.

THE ANOINTING OF JESUS' FEET

MONDAY OF HOLY WEEK.
6 April 2020 – Year A.

First Reading: Isaiah 42: 1-7
Responsorial Psalm: Psalm 27: 1, 2, 3, 13-14
Gospel: John 12: 1-11
HOMILY: Archbishop Charles Jason Gordon

Many scholars believe that the story of the Passion begins in Bethany with the anointing, the first of two anointing accounts in the Gospel that bookend the Passion. On one end, six days before the Passover, the anointing of Jesus' body in Bethany and on the other, the women going with Mary and some of the others to the tomb to anoint the body of Jesus on the morning of the Resurrection. And these two anointing events, these bookends, are really the beginning and end of the Passion.

In the first event, we have an anointing of the body, but in the second, there is no need because there is no body in the tomb to anoint. Our text today starts six days before the Passover, which means we are now down to a very focussed time where Jesus is going to give Himself. And, in the house, we have three characters that we know so well: Mary, Martha and Lazarus.

Lazarus, having been raised from the dead, is a source of distraction to Jesus and to the authorities because it means, if this man is alive, then Jesus is who He claims to be. Because nobody has ever raised anybody from death and certainly not after four days; it is giving credence to a thought in Israel that Jesus must be the Messiah. He must be the One that we are waiting on! And so, the Jewish establishment is nervous because of the life of Lazarus.

Isn't that interesting? That somebody who has experienced the amazing gift of having been brought back from death to life becomes a problem to somebody else – isn't that amazing? That somebody who has good fortune becomes a problem to somebody else; you do not find that a little bit weird? That somebody who has an unexpected, good turn of events leaves other people perturbed by it; do we do that at all? Any time? Where other people's good fortune somehow seems inconvenient to us and we not happy with it? We may not say it, but we may think it. This phenomenon with Lazarus is a very important phenomenon. It leads us to think of the times God has acted in the life of someone else and we have not been happy. Like in the story of the prodigal son, where the older son was angry with the father for receiving this wayward boy back into his home. We sometimes do not think the way God thinks!

But the story deepens. It goes on to talk about Mary who comes in the place where Jesus is and anoints Him with pure nard. They go on to say that the nard costs about 300 denarii. We know from another parable that a denarius is a day's wage; do the calculation with me! Let us say that a day's wage is $200; we would be talking about $60,000 worth of ointment! 300 days' worth of ointment! That is a significant amount of ointment. An excess, beyond excess, of ointment! This is generosity taken on steroids and carried to the extreme! But what is this generosity about? You see, because Mary had experienced the intervention of Jesus in raising her brother Lazarus from the dead, she experienced who

Jesus was. And in experiencing who Jesus was, there was no other response but to give back to God and to be extremely generous to God with everything she had.

One of the hallmarks of true spirituality is generosity. Gratitude and generosity go hand in hand. People who have really encountered God are people who are grateful and generous! If you have experienced God taking you from your stupidity and your waywardness – your "wotlessness" – and turning you around and bringing you back to know a love that is beyond every other love, if you have experienced that, you cannot be stingy with your love for God. And that is what we see in the text. In the first bookend of the Passion, Mary's generosity in anointing the body of Jesus is in preparation for what He will undergo, and she must anoint Him now because it is the last time His body will be anointed in preparation for His death. But this kind of thinking is contrasted with another kind – seemingly logical thinking – and that is the thinking of Judas.

What does Judas say? *"Well, you know, that nard should have been sold and the money given to the poor. Why are you wasting that kind of money on Him and on His body when the poor have such great need?"* Yeah, that is logical thinking, not so? Yet sometimes we think that way. Why do we decorate our churches the way we do? Why do we give lavishly to God the way that we do? And so, the generosity of Mary is a generosity that really challenges you and me because it is extreme generosity, really extreme generosity. Remember, Jesus had said to another woman, who washed His feet at Simon's house, that those who have been forgiven much, love much. It speaks about the depth of encounter with God which elicits a response of generosity from us.

You know, everybody has a thermometer these days; everybody is checking their temperature three times a day just to make sure it is okay. If you want a thermometer to check your spiritual health, look at your generosity. When you are being really generous, this is when you are connecting most deeply with God. When you go into practical reasoning and stinginess, you are disconnecting from God. More, too, is told of Judas, and John is the only one who tells us this: Judas was a thief. He would often help himself to the common purse, so the only reason he was so interested in the nard was for the money. There was no real, genuine concern for the poor, but rather, a genuine concern for his pocket because he was helping himself to the money in the common purse. This is a very important meditation; this is a meditation we must have.

Jesus kept Judas with Him up until the last. He ordained Judas as a priest knowing that Judas was betraying Him. For me, this is a most difficult meditation on the Passion: Jesus knew Judas was a thief and knew he was betraying Him, but He never gave up on Judas. He gave Judas every opportunity possible to turn back to Him and be converted. Every opportunity, up until the last. When we see sickness in the Church and we are terrified, remember Judas was at the Last Supper. Remember Jesus had him in charge of the common purse. Remember that he was not the character he should have been, but chose to sin in a particular way. And now, here, the drama of the Passion unfolds in this week.

Who do we want to be? Mary, responding out of extreme generosity? Or Judas, stuck in our sin-sickness? Are we unwilling to move from our sin-sickness, stuck in our own way of thinking, justifying our own way of thinking, and therefore, not moving, not being converted, not experiencing the amazing love of Jesus Christ? Here you have two characters: Mary of Bethany and Judas of Iscariot. Which one? Which one? The Judas character could not experience love, and because of that he could not experience conversion. The Mary character experiences love, and because of that she experiences conversion. The mystery of Holy Week and the invitation of today is that, whatever you have done in your life, wherever you have been, whatever foolishness you have done, however far you might be from God and whatever that might entail, do not do the Judas thing. Do the Mary thing! Come back to God. Open wide your heart to Him and say to Him, "I have sinned; I am in need of Your mercy. Have mercy on me, O God, for I have sinned against You." Do the Mary thing, become extremely generous with God. And allow that generosity to really fill you and take you through this Holy Week into the Easter Week. Amen.

THE BETRAYER IS REVEALED

TUESDAY OF HOLY WEEK.
07 April 2020 – Year A.

First Reading: Isaiah 49: 1-6
Responsorial Psalm: Psalm 71: 1-2, 3-4a, 5ab-6ab, 15 and 17
Gospel: John 13: 21-33, 36-38
HOMILY: Archbishop Charles Jason Gordon

During Holy Week, the Church uses the "Song of the Suffering Servant" texts from the Book of Isaiah for its first readings. Yesterday, we heard one from Isaiah 42, tomorrow we will hear Isaiah 50. And then, on Good Friday, we will hear that most terrifying of all the songs which speaks of the affliction of the Servant: "Like a sapling He grew up in front of us, like a root in arid ground." Today, we have the really incredible text of Isaiah 49.

When I was twenty years old, I was on retreat at Mount Saint Benedict. This passage came to me and, when it did, it changed something in me. It connected with me in a way that I could not believe at the time. And because of this passage, the whole direction of my life changed. "Islands, listen to me; pay attention remotest peoples. The Lord called me before I was born..." This gave me a sense that my vocation happened, not when I was twenty years old, but when I was in my mother's womb. And that every single one of us is called from our mother's womb for the purpose for which God intends us to live.

The Servant was called from his mother's womb and called for sacred purpose. You, too, have been called from your mother's womb and called for sacred purpose. That single fact just completely blew my mind! At twenty years old, I had never considered my life to have a purpose beyond my plans and the things I was engaged in. I was in business, I had eight people working for me; I was doing really well. I was happy. I had a lot of disposable income and, as a twenty-year-old, I was doing really, really nice. So, I never considered that my life had a sacred purpose; a purpose beyond the dream I had to become a millionaire. But this passage went inside of me and helped me to realign my life with an understanding which is absolute truth: that each of us has a sacred purpose, and our life is best when we are living that purpose!

This prophet was *made* to be a prophet! He said, *"I have made your mouth a sharpened sword...* He said to me: 'You are My servant Israel, in whom I shall be glorified'; while I was thinking, 'I have toiled in vain and I have exhausted myself for nothing.'" Very often, I have returned to this passage when I felt that I, too, have toiled in vain and exhausted myself for nothing. And I cannot see what God is really doing or what God is really asking, but I keep doing the things that I believe He is asking of me. How often in your life have you experienced a time of darkness where you are not sure what God is really asking, or saying, or directing of your life, but you do the things you believe are the right things to do? And then you find, "...All the while my cause was with the Lord, my reward was with my God. I was honoured in the eyes of the Lord and my God was my stronghold." He goes further, telling us more about what God says to him: "...He who formed me in the womb to be His servant, to bring back Jacob to Him, to gather Israel (said): 'It

134

is not enough for you to be my servant, to restore the tribes of Jacob and bring back the survivors of Israel…" – this text is about Jesus Christ.

From before He was in His mother's womb, from before the Annunciation, God called Him. And before the Annunciation, He chose to empty Himself and to become human in the flesh of Mary. And before all eternity, God chose Him to display what true love is and how true love comes to us. The Suffering Servant that Isaiah speaks about was fulfilled in Israel partially; this was because Israel was unable to gather all nations to itself. Israel remained believing that God was a God for the salvation of Israel only, not about using Israel for the salvation of the world. It is through Jesus Christ that salvation moves from Israel to all the nations: "Islands, listen to Me; pay attention remotest peoples." The Song of the Suffering Servant is a theology of salvation that is brought to us through Jesus Christ.

And we have the counterpart of this in the gospel today. Jesus was at Supper and Judas was at that Supper; I want you to contemplate this. Jesus knew about Judas and still had him at the Last Supper. He knew about Judas and still ordained him priest. He knew, and He still invited him to table fellowship. In ancient Israel to sit at table was a most intimate moment. Table fellowship meant a kind of intimacy that we do not have. It was not the individual chairs around a table that we are familiar with, but sitting down on the ground. You are propped up on one hand and use the other hand to feed yourself. And the only way to settle yourself is to lean into the person who is behind you, so that the person is leaning in to you and you are leaning in to them. This is intimacy like you have never had it. And in this most intimate moment where the Last Supper is unfolding, Jesus is giving Himself for our salvation; Judas is receiving the bread and goes out to betray. And Peter – who thinks he is "the bee's knees" and that he is better than everybody else – says, *"Lord, even if all of these foolish people betray you, not your boy, Peter!"* And hears Jesus say, *"Peter, you know, tonight, this very night, you will betray Me. You will betray Me!"*

The Last Supper is the greatest act of love we will ever understand in human terms. In this act Jesus betroths Himself to His bride, the Church, and consummates the marriage on Good Friday on the cross where, naked, He gives everything He has and gives His very body to us. On Holy Thursday, He gives His body and His blood to us. On Good Friday, naked, He gives himself totally for us and for our salvation. This is the mystery of sin and the mystery of evil. John says that the moment Judas ate the bread, Jesus told him to go and do what he had to do. And at that moment, too, when he ate the bread Satan entered him. So, it means that eating the Eucharist is not an antidote for our accepting evil. When we come to the table with evil intentions, evil is what springs forth. We have to come to the table with noble intentions, with a desire for God, with a desire for the things of God and to bend our hearts to the will of God. We have to come to the table bending our hearts, otherwise what springs forth will be what we see in Judas.

What is in your heart right now? What's churning in your heart? Are you in rhythm and in tune with God or in rebellion and angry with God? What is in your heart right now? As you come to this table, I invite you to bend your heart to Him. Let us not do like Judas. At the end of the passage John simply says: "And night fell." The darkness had come into the world. Do not let night fall on your mind or your heart, my mind or my heart. Let daylight, the light of Christ, shine. Let us bend our hearts. Let us bend our hearts to the will of God. He is the Suffering Servant, and you and I were saved by Him. Amen.

Thirty Silver Pieces

WEDNESDAY OF HOLY WEEK.
8 April 2020 – Year A.

First Reading: Isaiah 50: 4-9a
Responsorial Psalm: Psalm 69: 8-10, 21-22, 31 and 33-34
Gospel: Matthew 26: 14-25
HOMILY: Archbishop Charles Jason Gordon

Today is called "Spy Wednesday". Do you know why? Because Judas went about spying to see how to betray Jesus. And so, tradition calls this Spy Wednesday because it is here that the plot gets thick. It is here that the whole bacchanal starts breaking out. It is night when the betrayal is set in motion and the whole scene put into action. Judas – and we do not get a motive – went to the chief priests and asked what they were prepared to give him for handing Jesus over to them. Matthew's Gospel, therefore, makes Judas into a mercenary. He did not go for an ideological reason, a disagreement with Jesus. He did not go for an emotive reason, a reason of passion. It was for money that he hands over Jesus. And we see other things in other gospels that give us other clues into the motive. But the real question is: why are you and I handing over Jesus? Why are we? For what good purpose? What gain do we think we could have?

Do you think if Judas could have seen history from our vantage point, he would have made the choice he made on that day, handing Jesus over? Well, why do we betray Jesus? Why do we betray the poor into poverty and do nothing about it? That is handing over Jesus again. When we betray the lonely and we do nothing about it – that is handing over

Jesus again. When we betray those on the margins of society and we allow them to be condemned to whatever they are living through while we are prospering – that is handing Him over again. Our faith is a social faith; it is not about "me and my Jesus." And we have never been allowed to be "me and my Jesus" people because Jesus, if He did anything at all, incorporated us into His whole body. And so, what one member of the body feels, the whole body feels. And that started not with the Church; that started with Israel.

Our first reading says, "The Lord has given me a disciple's tongue. So that I may know how to reply to the wearied, he provides me with speech. Each morning, he wakes me to hear, to listen like a disciple. The Lord has opened my ear." And the whole meditation in Isaiah 50, which is the Third Song of the Suffering Servant, is the meditation of a disciple who wants to know the will of God, wants to do the will of God and will go to any end or extreme to put the will of God into practice. So, the Lord gives him a tongue to speak, an ear to listen: "Each morning, he wakes me to hear." "The Lord has opened my ear." "For my part, I made no resistance and neither did I turn away." How many of us could say that?

You know how much resistance I make to poor God! I feel sorry for Him all the time for the number of times I resist Him! What resistance are we putting up to God right now? Judas put up his resistance, and he went to betray Jesus for thirty pieces of silver. What resistance are you putting up to God right now? How are you resisting God? What is God asking of you that you are unwilling to give? What is He asking you? And if we could locate that resistance today, in locating it, we might understand the way that we are participating in the drama of this incredible time.

The text goes on to say: "I offered my back for those who struck me, my cheeks for those who tore at my beard. I did not cover my face against insult and spittle." That means there is a suffering to be had by the disciple. And, often, this is the one thing that gets us scared, yes? If there is a big turn-off in discipleship, this is it. We want discipleship, but we do not want the suffering. We want to be with Jesus in heaven, but we do not want the cross. But what the Isaiah text is telling us is that this disciple who was completely attuned to God, who listened and spoke as God dictated, whose heart was turned to God, this disciple would suffer. And that is why it is called the "Song of the Suffering Servant".

This suffering is exactly what Jesus experienced: "I offered my back to those who struck me, my cheeks to those who tore at my beard. I did not cover my face against insult and spittle." This is a disciple because he has put his trust in the Lord, and said the Lord comes to his help so that he is untouched by the insults. "So, too, I set my face like flint; I know I shall not be put to shame." And here, we have the other half of the drama of this incredible week. Judas is spying out a way to betray Jesus, and Jesus is silent. There is an inner serenity in Him. You hear it in this text. Jesus is not flustered, not worried, not bothered. In the gospel text, He is treating Judas like He is treating everybody else and hoping that Judas would come to his senses. Jesus has a calm in Him; Judas has an agitation in him. And that is the drama.

Where are you? In the calm or the agitation? We are facing this pandemic, COVID-19, and if you have not heard the message before: stay in your house, do not go out; stay there unless it is absolutely urgent for you to move. And in your house, find a calm. Find that place where you can hear as a disciple hears, where you can speak as a disciple speaks, where your whole spirit is centered as a disciple's spirit is centered. Find that place. But to find that place you may have to discover the places where you are resisting God. We have to find the resistance to God that is in our heart. Judas resisted, and we know where that led. Where is your resistance right now? Ask God in this Mass, as a grace of this Eucharist, to show you where that resistance is. Because if you can find that resistance to God, you can offer it to Him and He can make you free. And then we, too, like the disciple can listen, can speak and can put our whole trust in God. Amen.

THE TRIDUUM

THE SACRIFICE OF THE LAMB

HOLY THURSDAY.
9 April 2020 – Year A.

First Reading: Exodus 12: 1-8, 11-14
Responsorial Psalm: Psalm 116: 12-13, 15-16bc, 17-18
Second Reading: 1 Corinthians 11: 23-26
Gospel: John 13: 1-15
HOMILY: Archbishop Charles Jason Gordon

During the Jewish celebration of Passover, a little child asks: "Why is this night different from every other night?" On every other night we have a congregation, and on this night, we have none. On every other night in this Cathedral, we have altar servers, pomp and ceremony. On this night we have none. But we have something on this night that is different and special from other nights; on this night we have our priests together with us. You will see them from time to time during this broadcast in their own chapel, at their own altar, sitting and celebrating with us. And, together, we are offering this Mass for you, for every parish in the diocese. We are offering Mass for you, the people of God in Trinidad and Tobago.

Tonight, we celebrate what is most precious. We celebrate the Institution of the Eucharist, the Institution of the Priesthood and the conviction of love which Jesus showed by giving of Himself in the Last Supper and by washing of the feet, showing that a leader's true love is humble service.

In our Second Reading, St. Paul says to the Corinthians at the very end of verse 26 that, whenever you celebrate the bread and the wine, the body and the blood of Christ, you are remembering the Lord's Passover, you are remembering the Lord's death. Whenever you celebrate the Eucharist you are remembering the Lord's death. He said this because the people of Corinth were celebrating Eucharist in a way that was just so haphazard – sometimes they understood, sometimes they did not. They came together and were feasting and having a great time, but not understanding what they were celebrating. This desert that we have been in because of COVID has forced us to ask the question: what do we celebrate when we celebrate Eucharist? The fast from the Eucharist that we have had is asking another question of us: What do we come to Church for? What are we celebrating?

There is a wonderful story by Matthew Kelly in his teaching on Eucharist. He says, imagine we have – (COVID-19!) – a major viral plague that infected the whole world. And for this infection, doctors realise that there is an antivirus they could have, but they need the blood of a very special person to be able to make that antivirus to inoculate the whole world. And so, all over the world they are looking to find this cure, this one person, who has this specific type of blood that could help in inoculating and saving the whole world. Everywhere in the world, doctors and labs are looking and searching for this one person. Then your family goes to be checked in the clinic, and you realise that people who checked in after you are leaving, but you are not. You realise that something is wrong. And then the doctors come to you in a hurry and say: "You know, your son has the cure that can save everyone. Your little boy, five years old, his blood is the only one they found, so far, throughout the whole world that can save everyone. Would you sign here and give us permission to take his blood?" "So how much blood do you need?" "Well, actually, we thought we would get an adult, but this is a little child so we will need all of his blood." You are torn. What do you do? If you do not sign, everybody dies; if you sign, you lose your son. What do you do? So eventually, you sign, reluctantly, and you do not even get the time to say goodbye to him. They take him, they take his blood, they find the cure, everybody is inoculated, everybody is cured – the world is saved because of your son. One month later, they have a little celebration for this heroic boy who gave his life and, when the celebration is to take place, very few people come and those who do, come more out of curiosity. They come, but there is no real gratitude. They come, and there is no real connection. They come, and they are just there, while you are still in grief because you have lost your son. The whole world has gone on with its business as if it were just another day – and that is the best way of trying to understand what St. Paul is saying. Whenever we celebrate the Eucharist we celebrate the Passion and Death of Jesus Christ. Why? Because every time we come to the Eucharistic table, we are celebrating *"eucharistia"* – "thanksgiving". Each time, we come to offer thanksgiving because God showed us what true love is. And in showing us true love, He is showing the gift of His Son to you and to me, for through His blood we have been saved.

During this Triduum, follow the blood! Follow the blood! To follow the blood, we have to go back to Egypt, to our first reading where the people were enslaved and God delivered them. And in that deliverance, He said, take a lamb, a young lamb, unblemished, and slaughter it. Take the blood and smear the doorposts of your houses. Roast that lamb, gather your families around and eat the lamb. As families you must eat all of it. And so, the people, on that night before they left Egypt, got their lambs, slaughtered their lambs, roasted their lambs, ate their lambs and put blood on the doorposts of their houses. The angel of death passed over and, then, God said to the people, *"Every year, I want you to remember."*

Now, the word "remember" here is not the same as "memory". It is not a calling to mind, a recollection. It is *re-membering*, which is stepping into the event as if you were there in Egypt yourself, as if God personally delivered you Himself and set you free from slavery to a life of grace, to the Promised Land. In this recollection, in this memorial, it is not just a mental but a spiritual re-enactment of the saving events that the people went through when they were in Egypt.

Paul tells us: *"What I have learnt, I pass on to you: that on the night before He died, Jesus took bread and said the blessing, He broke the bread and gave it to His disciples saying, 'Take this, all of you, and eat; do this in memory of Me.' And He took the cup, He said the blessing, He gave it to them and said, 'This is the blood of the new covenant...'"* The new covenant; blood of the new covenant. Why is this the blood of the new covenant? Because by the Eucharist, the old covenant has been superseded and this new covenant emerges. And this is what is at the heart of the Eucharist – that God has made a loving pact with you and me. And the price of that loving pact is the offering of His Son – Body, Blood, Soul and Divinity – for you and for me. Each time we come to the Eucharist, we are celebrating what Jesus Christ did. So, when He says, *"Do this in memory of Me"*, it is not a call on your memory. It is putting yourself in that sacred scene, in active imagination, at that Last Supper where He was, seeing yourself sitting there, being there, as He gave His body as bread and His blood as wine. And it is understanding that what He did that night, He does again tomorrow when He gives His body and His blood is poured out.

On the day of the Last Supper, all of Jerusalem was in a frenzy to celebrate the Passover. All the families would go to the temple to get a lamb and carry it to the priest, who would kill that lamb and drain its blood into the canal right up by the altar. And then the priest would stretch that lamb out and tie its hooves out so that it was tied in a crucified form. Jehoshaphat, one of the Jewish writers, tells us that, in Jerusalem, 270,000 lambs were slaughtered. 270,000 lambs slaughtered! And all in the sign of a cross! And also, in Jerusalem that year, there was one unblemished Lamb that was slaughtered. And that one unblemished Lamb, Jesus Christ, gave Himself for you and for me.

The mystery that we are celebrating is a mystery of deep wisdom. It is a mystery of deep gratitude. I would like you to consider what God has done for you through His Son, Jesus Christ. Consider the price that He paid. Every time we eat the Body and Blood of Christ, we celebrate His crucifixion and His death. We remember it so that we are thankful for what God has done for us. Until this time of COVID-19, we thought we were okay, we thought our life was okay and we really did not need God. But now, we are seeing it a little differently – very, very differently.

Tonight is very strange for all of our priests. As priests, Holy Thursday is the day that we renew our promise of priesthood. We usually do it a little earlier on the Monday or Tuesday of the week so that people can get back to their parishes. But it is on this day, Holy Thursday, that we commit ourselves every year to the priesthood and to the priestly vows we made when we were ordained. It is on Holy Thursday that we remember the Institution of the Priesthood and the ordination of these first priests. It is on Holy Thursday that we remember it was at the Institution of the Eucharist that God gave Himself as bread for you and for me. It is on Holy Thursday that we remember the Washing of the Feet, although, this year we cannot wash feet.

So we remember that Jesus came as a humble servant, a very humble servant. A covenant in blood has been made and a covenant is a contract. Today, you have lawyers preparing contracts and, when the contract is signed, you know that it is binding, otherwise they would take you to court. In the ancient days, they did not do it that way. They did a covenant in blood, because the covenant basically stated that if you break this covenant, your blood may also be spilled. It was as drastic as that. The blood that was spilled in this covenant was not the blood of goats or sheep; it was the blood of Jesus Christ! And that blood was spilled for you and for me. Each time we celebrate the Eucharist, we remember the Passion of Jesus Christ and we remember the high cost He paid for our salvation.

Pray for your priests today! I am asking you, wherever you are, to pray for your priest. Whichever priest is in your parish, as a family pray for him tonight and in these times. Remember, Trinidad and Tobago, all of our priests gathered virtually throughout the archdiocese are offering our Mass today for you, for your families, for this nation, for the people. Also, remember the Mass is a celebration of thanksgiving, and we should come with grateful hearts to God, to thank God for what God has done for us. Let us reflect today on the attitude and disposition that we come with to the Mass. How often have we come and were bored or unimpressed but, really, had not prepared ourselves to come? How often we have come and not invested, not been grateful for what God has done for us? Let us, today, turn to this great Lord, who gives everything that He has, that you and I may find life in Him. Amen.

THE CRUCIFIXION AND DEATH OF OUR LORD

GOOD FRIDAY.
10 April 2020 – Year A.

First Reading: Isaiah 52: 13 – 53: 12
Responsorial Psalm: Psalm 31: 2, 6, 12-13, 15-16, 17, 25
Second Reading: Hebrews 4: 14-16; 5: 7-9
Gospel: John 18: 1 – 19: 42
HOMILY: Archbishop Charles Jason Gordon

"Who could believe what we have heard, and to whom has the power of the Lord been revealed? Like a sapling he grew up in front of us, like a root in arid ground. Without beauty…to attract our eyes."

When Isaiah penned his most famous Fourth Song of the Suffering Servant, he could never have imagined the ways in which it would be fulfilled. He could not have imagined that the text would be fulfilled so completely in the scenes before our eyes on this Good Friday. He would never have believed that this text would unfold with the Son of God being taken and treated brutally. He would never have imagined how the fulfillment of that text would bring both a sense of hope, because God's word had prophesied the things that we behold, and a sense of calm because it meant that God was involved in this. God was involved in this!

On the night before Jesus died, He celebrated the Supper, then He went to the garden, sweat blood and tears and said, *"Father, Father, take this cup away from Me."* Today, He has drunk the chalice, He has drunk deep from the chalice of suffering – the second baptism that He has undergone –

all the many ways in which His body has been disfigured by the flagellation, the thirty-nine lashes He would have received, the spitting, the crown of thorns, the many who would beat Him and hit Him on every side. All the many ways that His body would have been disfigured during this incredible scene, and as He lays bare before our eyes and we look at this scene, how do we make sense of this suffering?

For a moment, I invite you to ponder Mary; Mary, who is moving with the crowd. Find that opportunity to meet Him. Mary heard the words of the angel that she was to conceive a child and He would be named Jesus, Son of the Most High. Mary knows what the angel said. Yet, Mary is here, looking at her Son being completely disfigured in front of her eyes, rejected. And yes, she also would have remembered Simeon's words, "…a sword shall pierce your own soul too, so that the secret thoughts of many may be laid bare." That sword pierced her soul on that Good Friday.

As we enter into these events, it is so difficult to comprehend what it must have been for the followers of Jesus in that first crucifixion scene to behold what they saw, to understand what unfolded before their eyes. We hear from John's account today that blood and water flowed from Jesus' side after He died. John is making a theological reference here, because when John is speaking about the blood and water flowing from Jesus' side, he is speaking about two sacraments – the Sacrament of the Eucharist and the Sacrament of Baptism – that flow from the side of Christ. Follow the blood! Remember on the Passover Day, when the 270,000 lambs would have been slain in the temple near the altar, the blood of the lambs would have been flowing in the canals of the altar, out of the side of the altar, out of the side of the temple. So, if you were in the Kedron Valley, what you would have seen that day was blood and water flowing from the side of the temple. John is making this reference to say that Jesus is the new temple. Remember Jesus said, "Destroy this temple and, in three days, I will rebuild it." Jesus is the new temple. And if He is the new temple, He is the new altar. That is why the Second Vatican Council says that Christ is present in the liturgy. He is present in the people who are gathered because we are the body of Christ. He is present in the Word, he is present in the priest, he is present in the altar and he is pre-eminently present in the Blessed Sacrament.

Last night, when I stripped the altar, it was to shock us into the reality that the altar, which is a symbol of Christ, is being stripped. Having celebrated the Last Supper, Christ moved forward from that moment to this, where His body would be stripped and He would be laid bare. Normally, we dress up our altar, but today He lays bare before us. Today He has nothing to hide Him. Consider your reaction when you saw that altar stripped. Consider what happened in your heart and in your soul. Consider, for a moment, the shock or horror or terror or wonder or whatever emotion it was and ask yourself, do you feel that way when we strip the body of Christ, the Church? When we treat her badly? When we speak of her badly? When we spread falsehood or scandal about her? Do we feel the same shock and horror when we malign the body of Christ?

Remember what Jesus said to Paul on the way to Damascus: "Why are you persecuting Me?" "Who are You, Lord?" "I am Jesus, and you are persecuting Me." Paul, persecuting the Church, was persecuting the body of Jesus

Christ. Do we feel that same shock and horror when we strip each other? And you know how good we are at stripping each other! "Giving picong", making supposedly funny remarks that tear people down in front of other people. And the way we strip each other in our families, making fun of the weaknesses of family members so that they are shamed into submission and do not feel as if they are people who have worth and dignity. Are we shocked when we are stripping each other? Are we still shocked?

Are we shocked when we are stripping the earth, when we treat creation so badly – this incredible gift that God has given to us? Are we in shock at the plastics that we have created that end up in the oceans and in the rivers and waterways? Are we in shock with what we have done to the earth? Are we shocked by it? We should be shocked! Because if we are shocked at how the body of Jesus Christ is being treated, if we are shocked at how the altar and its cloths are being treated, then brothers and sisters, I pray we have the sensitivity to be shocked at how we are treating each other. Because Christ is being crucified again, and again, and again, and you and I are the source of the crucifixion. One of the Fathers of the Church stated that every time we sin, we crucify Christ again. Every time we sin, we nail Him to the cross. Every time we sin, we condemn Him one more time. Brothers and sisters, you and I have crucified Jesus Christ. Let us be shocked this day at the way that we treat one another.

On the night before He died, Jesus prayed: *"Let them be one, Father, as you and I are one."* This is the prayer of a dying man for His Church. Are we shocked when we break the unity of the Church and act in a way that brings disharmony and disunity? Are we shocked at that? Are we shocked when we break down the unity within our parish, or within our family, or within the Church as a whole? Are we shocked at that? The crucifixion is a case for shock and scandal, and we should be shocked! We should be scandalised! But, because we have read it so often, because our hearts have become so accustomed to hearing it, because we have seen it so many times, it does not shock us any more. Today, I want you to be shocked and scandalised at our action of crucifying Jesus Christ. Let us be shocked and scandalised at the way we treat the poor in our country, because He says, "I came to you hungry, naked, in prison..." Are we shocked at how we treat our prisoners? Because that, too, is the body of Christ being crucified here in Trinidad and Tobago every single day!

Brothers and sisters, "Who could believe what we have heard, to whom has the power of God been revealed? Like a sapling He grew up in front of us, like a root in arid ground." And yet this One, whom we threw all our negativity upon, this same One, what He throws back at us is love: "Father forgive them; they know not what they do." From His cross, having absorbed all the pain that the cross has to give, He forgives us. In our reading today, His last words are His most precious: "It is accomplished." It is accomplished! The mission that God had given to Him is now accomplished. He has reconciled the world to Himself and to God. It is accomplished! The mission that God had given to Him to show broken humanity the way of love. It is accomplished! Because the cross is not just the source of horror and scandal, it is the most profound image of love that we will ever know on our earth. Consider what love is: Jesus

Christ on the cross enduring great pain, horror and scandal, and still being able to say, "I love you." That is Jesus Christ and that is what the cross says. The cross says, "Despite every shock, horror, scandal that you have thrown upon Me, I love you." And that is why the cross is a symbol of love.

One of the traditions in scripture interpretation says, "It is consummated." And that makes the point really, really clear. Because the ancient Fathers believed that the relationship between Christ and the Church was of Bridegroom and Bride. This ancient understanding, where Christ is seen as the bridegroom, is how John the Baptist introduces Him and we see this in so many texts in our gospels. When Jesus says, "It is consummated", what He is saying is that this nuptial relationship between Him and His Church is consummated. He has shown the Church what real love is. And now that this love is consummated, now that He has given everything for you and for me, He asks us to love as He loved. He asks us to become as He was. He asks us to have a heart that is open to the fragile, to the poor, to the vulnerable. "It is consummated."

God, through Jesus Christ, has reconciled the whole world to Himself. This is Good News, that we have been reconciled. Today on this Good Friday, in this day of scandal and shock and horror, let us recognise the ways that we have added scandal to the scandal of the cross right here in Trinidad and Tobago, right here in our families, right here in our society – the ways that we have added to the scandal of the cross. And let us bow our heads before our God and recognise His incredible love for us and say to Him: "Jesus, I trust in You. Jesus, have mercy on me; I trust in You. Jesus, forgive me, forgive me through the blood of Your cross, because I trust in You." Let us recognise that the mystery of the cross is central to the whole of salvation. Today, embrace Him, the Crucified One. As you embrace Him, see the ways that you, too, have crucified Jesus Christ.

HE IS RISEN

HOLY SATURDAY – Easter Vigil.
11 April 2020 – Year A.

Frist Reading: Romans 6: 3-11
Responsorial Psalm: Psalm 118: 1-2, 16-17, 22-23
Gospel: Matthew 28: 1-10
HOMILY: Archbishop Charles Jason Gordon

What a preparation for this night we have had! We have had forty days in a desert – yeah, the COVID-19 desert. A Lent on steroids like no other Lent! A Triduum, like no other Triduum that we have ever had. And tonight, we have come to where we make the Easter proclamation: "Christ our Lord is risen from the dead! He is risen as He said He would!" And as we proclaim the Resurrection of the Risen Lord, we proclaim that death has no power over us any more, that life will break forth and light will be triumphant! But let us make the journey again. Let us journey back through the Triduum to recap and recount how we have moved from place to place, so that we can understand the sacred mystery of this special night where we proclaim that the light has come into the darkness and illumines the darkness; although the darkness does not like the light.

Through the forty days, plunged into the desert, we journeyed steadfastly. On Thursday night, we celebrated the Paschal Mystery of Ordination with all our priests joining us on Zoom, as they did last night, as they do tonight. And on Thursday night, as the altar was stripped, people gasped. They told me last night, "I thought you went mad!" "I wanted to call to find out if you were okay." But, the stripping of the altar was the stripping of Jesus Christ, Himself. Because that night, after He left the Last Supper, He went into the Garden of Gethsemane and He was stripped.

But you would have noticed, too, in the Good Friday liturgy that the bishop was also stripped. To approach the cross, I took off mitre, I took off chasuble, I took off everything. I took off my shoes to approach the cross, because the bishop strips down to approach the cross. Because the only way that we can come to the cross, is if we are stripped down. And the bishop, representing the apostles, enters into the mystery as they did, because on that night, they were stripped. They believed that Jesus was going into Jerusalem to conquer as a mighty triumphant hero and they wanted places of honour, but nothing prepared them for the scandal of the cross. Everything they believed was stripped away from them. Everything was violently wrenched from them. Every last hope that they held to was violently dragged away from them as they saw the nights unfolding, as they saw Friday unfold and as they saw Jesus being condemned to death like a common criminal, taking His cross with Him.

But after the death of Jesus, where did the apostles go? Where did they gather? Where did they come together? We learn from scripture that they huddled in the Upper Room. And it was the providence of Jesus for His disciples when, before the Passover, they asked Him where they should spend the Passover and He said to them, *"Go into the city, to So-and-So's place, and you will see such and such, and say to them that the Master wants a place for His Passover."* So that is where they went. They huddled in the Upper Room. And the disciples huddled in the Upper Room dejected, filled with fear, hopelessness and with a sense of guilt and shame for their own sinfulness and weakness. They stayed there that night and this day. And I want you to imagine, for a moment, when Mary came into that Upper Room after having been given over to John as his Mother. She comes into that Upper Room to these fellas who have betrayed her Son, who have denied Him, run away from Him – how does Mary greet them? How does she treat with them? They are stripped; they had nothing more to give. But Mary gives each one courage. Each one, she forgives. Each one, she prepares for what will happen next. We were living in the desert for forty days, but we have moved location now. For the next forty days, we are going to live in the Upper Room.

Because it is in the Upper Room that the first community was formed. It is in the Upper Room that the disciples come to the truth and the fullness of the faith. It is in the Upper Room, over those forty days, that the disciples encounter Jesus Christ many times and it is in the Upper Room that they come to understand what the Easter proclamation really means: they need not have fear any more. It is in the Upper Room that they understand that Christ the Lord is risen from the dead as He said He would. So, we are moving location! We are no longer in the desert. I call the whole Church of Trinidad and Tobago to the Upper Room! That is where we will be over this time, because this is where Mary formed the disciples and they prepared themselves for the mission which they will have after Pentecost.

So, between now and Pentecost, there is a formation that is going on. Between now and Pentecost, there is a revelation that is taking place. Between now and Pentecost, the understanding of the Resurrection is slowly unveiling in their minds and hearts. And here lies the mystery for you and for me: we can only understand the Resurrection if we are prepared to be stripped, if we are prepared to let go of all we thought was so valid and so important to all of us. We can only enter into this incredible mystery, if we have gone – as Jesus did, as the Apostles did, as the Early Church did – to be stripped of everything that we think so grand and important in our lives. To enter into this mystery of the Resurrection, we have to be stripped, and we have to allow ourselves to be stripped, and that is what COVID-19 has given to us as a gift. It has stripped us of our rat race. It has stripped us of our importance. It has stripped us of our grandiose self and our egotism. It has stripped us of believing that we are so important and that we have no need for God. It has stripped us of our illusion that God has no part in a modern world. It has stripped us of the belief that science will solve all of our problems. It has stripped us of our faith in science, as if science can be more important to us than God! And Christ is stripping us still. It is only through this stripping, and allowing ourselves to be stripped, that we will dare to see and perceive this message of the Resurrection and it will become clearer and clearer to us as we live these days in the Upper Room.

The disciples lived in their Upper Room, and many times we meet them there as the text would say, "They were in the Upper Room, locked away for fear of the Jews." We can say that differently: "We are in the Upper Room locked away, with the doors locked tight for fear of COVID-19." We are in an Upper Room, but here is the thing that we need to see and hear. In this Upper Room, the disciples were filled with *fear*. They were filled with *guilt* and remorse that they had betrayed their Saviour, their Master, and had run away at the most crucial moment; they knew their sin and their weakness. They were filled with guilt because they knew what they did was wrong and they were filled with *hopelessness*. I want you to hear those four characteristics, because those are the four powers that the devil uses to rob us of our joy, the four powers that the devil uses to snatch us from Christ, the four powers that he uses to undermine us. But it is on this night of the Resurrection that those four powers will give way to the light that is Jesus Christ.

The first thing that the two women hear in the garden as they go is: "Do not be afraid." Do not be afraid! As I talk to people in this pandemic, fear is the most consistent response that people are having. Think of the kind of fear you have been living in the last week or two or three or four. Think of the fear that has totally consumed you. And I want you to hear from Jesus Christ, Himself, tonight: "Do not be afraid." Do not be afraid, because you have gone down into the waters of baptism with Jesus Christ and you have died with Christ, and because you have died with Christ: "Death where is your sting? Death where is your victory?" As we have heard from the Letter to the Romans today, if we have died with Christ, we will rise with Christ in glory. The stripping we have experienced is one part of the mystery of the renewal of the Church in Trinidad and Tobago and in the Caribbean and in the world, of wherever you are joining us from. That is the first part of the mystery.

The other part of the mystery is the light of the Resurrection. Because in this Upper Room, as they experienced fear, Jesus said to them: "Do not be afraid." Do not be afraid! Tonight, in our reading from Matthew, as the two women go to the tomb, what do they see? Who moved the stone? Who moved that stone? That big boulder that they knew they could not move! Yet they went towards that grave with some form of hope that, somehow, the stone would be moved by somebody. And, who moved it? God, Himself, moved that stone! And God will move the stone in front of your heart to open your graves and allow the Resurrection light to fill every area of your life if you let Him. But we must hear the words of the angel to the women: "Do not be afraid." Because this COVID virus may kill our bodies, but it cannot kill our souls! It may wreak havoc on our world economy, but it cannot kill our spirit and our faith in Jesus Christ. Do not be afraid of that which can kill the body. Fear Him, rather, who can take our souls to heaven with Him in glory! Many times, sin – and you know the way that sin clings so closely to us – can make us feel unworthy of God because of our sin-sickness and because we know what we have done is so wrong. Where there is fear, Jesus gives love and where there is sin, He gives forgiveness. And tonight, I ask you to go before Jesus Christ, the Risen Lord, with your sin. You tell Him that sin, you ask for mercy tonight. Allow the light of the Resurrection to shine inside of that sin-sick area in your life and allow the Resurrection light to light up your life.

Guilt was the third of the powers. Guilt is when we are distorted and out of harmony with ourselves, with God, with our neighbour and with creation. Where there is guilt, He gives reconciliation, and tonight, Jesus Christ is reconciling the world to Himself. You and I are the agents of this reconciliation and I say to you, on behalf of God: "Be reconciled to God!" Because in our reconciliation with God, we will be reconciled to each other, to ourselves, to the creation and to every living being. Be reconciled to God!

And the fourth of these great powers is the one that has wreaked the worst havoc upon us: despair and hopelessness. Think of the hopelessness you have experienced because of COVID-19 – think about it. Think of that hopelessness that the disciples experienced in the Upper Room after Jesus had been put to death. Think of the despair and the way in which their hopes had been dashed. We see a glimpse of it when we meet the men on their way to Emmaus; they said their hopes had been dashed, because they had hoped Jesus would restore Israel. And what the disciples experienced in the Upper Room between last night and tonight, is what you and I have been experiencing for the last forty days when this COVID virus took a hold of Trinidad and Tobago, coming from China, through the rest of the world, to us. On Friday March 13th, 2020, we had to lock down the Church, so there has been no service since then and that has brought despair to so many people. I want to say, as your Shepherd, and I want you to hear me with everything inside of you: Do not despair! Put your hope in Jesus Christ, because He has conquered death and He brings life where there is death and hope where there is despair. It is Jesus Christ who opens life and allows life to flow again.

I want to say a special word to a special group throughout the archdiocese who are suffering in a big way tonight. You were to be baptised tonight. You were looking forward to becoming a Catholic on this night. You prepared for two years for this Easter night, when you would come to the waters of Baptism. When this Easter flame would be lit, when this light of Christ would be lit, and plunged into the waters, making it holy so that you, passing through the waters of Baptism, would move from death to life. To you I say this night, as the whole Church renews its baptismal promises, I ask you to make an Act of Faith with us and to beg God tonight for a Baptism of Desire, beg Him for a Baptism of Desire. Desire baptism more than life itself, and allow the Lord – who supplies for the Church every grace that is required for the Church which she cannot supply herself – to supply you tonight with the grace of baptism through a desire in your heart. The Church teaches that there is Baptism of Desire; desire tonight that you will be united with Jesus Christ. And we will make every haste to bring you through the baptismal font to the light of Christ which is Jesus, Himself.

Tonight is like no other night. But tonight, understand the power of the Resurrection. We must first empty ourselves and be stripped. We have had many opportunities of stripping, many opportunities of being tugged and flung to pieces, but tonight, let us allow this infilling of Christ. Christ who was not conquered by death, whom the grave could not hold; the stone could not keep Him in, but was rolled so that He could come out victorious! The Resurrection is not simply the proof that Jesus is God; it is the *action* of God. And that is why the reading starts in Matthew by saying it was the day "after the Sabbath… the first day of the week." It was on the first day of the week, as we also heard in our first reading, that God said: "'Let there be light' and there was light." The light shattered the darkness; darkness cannot overpower the light. Where there was fear, He showed them love. Where there was sin, He gave forgiveness. Where there was guilt, He offered reconciliation. And where there was hopelessness, He gave them hope. To the Church, the archdiocese, the region, to those of you who participate in these sacred mysteries with me, the gift that Jesus wants to give us tonight is the gift of love, the gift of forgiveness, the gift of reconciliation and the gift of hope – through these we will have the gift of faith. But we know the greatest, the greatest of these, is love. I beg you this night, open wide your heart! Do not stay in the tomb where Jesus died. Do not do like the women, going to visit the tomb where He was buried, because Jesus Christ is alive! Let us, as a Church, be alive with Him! Amen.

ADDENDUM: CHRISM MASS

THE CLEANSING OF THE TEMPLE

Chrism Mass:
Feast of the Dedication of the Lateran Basilica in Rome.
Monday November 9, 2020.

First Reading: Ezekiel 47: 1-2, 8-9, 12
Responsorial Psalm: Psalm 46: 2-3, 5-6, 8-9
Second Reading: 1 Corinthians 3: 9-11, 16-17
Gospel: John 2: 13-22
HOMILY: Archbishop Charles Jason Gordon

The Dedication of the Lateran Basilica in Rome is a feast that started in Rome. After a time, it was then spread to the Universal Church. Built during the pontificate of Pope Melchiades (311-314), it's the most ancient church in the world. In the early days, it was both his residence and his cathedral, and it is where the *"cathedra"*, the chair of the Pope, resides. We often think of St. Peter's Basilica as the first church of the Pope, but this honour remains with St. John Lateran. Whenever the Holy Father makes an official pronouncement *"ex cathedra"* meaning, "from the chair", it is at the Cathedral of St. John Lateran. This church is the mother of all the cathedrals of the world and the cathedral is the mother of all the churches in a diocese; this is like the mother of all mothers! It is celebrated throughout the world as a major feast because it reminds us of something that is so important in these days.

To celebrate St. John Lateran is to recognise the primacy of the Holy Father as first among bishops of the world. And as the first of equals, he holds the office of unity. As such, St. John Lateran Basilica holds the office of unity as a symbol of the unity of the Church. As we look to St. John Lateran Basilica, we celebrate also our own cathedral here in Port of Spain which was dedicated on this day.

The unity of the Church is what Jesus prayed for the night before He died: "Father, may they be one as you and I are one." And praying for unity on the night before He died, Jesus put unity square and centre, determining that unity would be why and how people would believe Jesus is God. So, there is no evangelisation without unity and that is why the Church sees unity as a sacrament; the Church is a sacrament of unity. A sacrament of harmony because in the beginning, in the Garden, there was harmony and that harmony was broken by sin. The Church is the agent of God to bring back the unity which existed in the beginning; it is through the Church that this unity goes out into the world.

Our first reading from the Book of Ezekiel is a wonderful and incredible text. In this text, we have a typology, and what we know from the Old Testament typology is that the type is a pre-figuring of the reality. But the type also holds, in essence and in a diminished way, what the reality would hold and fully reveal. And so, the reality is always more potent, more powerful, more real than that which the type is pre-figuring. And if you listen to the Ezekiel text on the beautiful stream, what we have is a typology of the Church. The stream which flowed from the sanctuary went out, and each time it was measured, it went deeper. It was measured four times, and it was deeper and deeper and deeper. And eventually, the stream flowed into the Dead Sea and then into the big sea, and wherever the stream went there was healing. The waters of the stream brought healing to the waters of the Dead Sea; the Dead Sea that was incapable of producing any form of life was healed when the waters of the sanctuary flowed into it. There were trees on either side of the stream and they were fruitful; they bore every month. And not only were the trees fruitful, their leaves were medicinal and brought healing to the world. This is the typology of the Church, because in Jerusalem on that fateful day, water flowed from the side of the temple, from the side of Christ.

We have the gospel reading now where Jesus said, "Destroy this temple and in three days I will rebuild it." He was speaking about His own body. And so, from His body – the temple, the true temple, not the typology, but the real, living temple on the cross, demonstrating what true love is in total sacrifice and total self-giving – from His side flows water and that water is the healing of the nations. That water, when it flows even into the Dead Sea, would bring life again. And when that water flows into all the parts of the world, life will flow and flourishing will happen. To see the typology of Ezekiel in the body of Jesus is to understand, brothers, that we have been entrusted with something that is so sacred, something that is so real, something that is so true that we should be shivering before the mysteries that we stand before every single day.

The Fathers of the Church have always interpreted the water from the side of Christ and the beautiful stream of Ezekiel as the waters of Baptism. They have also seen the trees on either bank of the stream as the fruit or the teachings of the Church in the Old and New Testaments – the word of

God given for the healing of the nations. And that is why every leaf is medicinal, because every part of scripture, every part of scripture brings to life that which was dead and brings to hope that which was hopeless.

To go deeper into the typology of the stream as a type of the Church, we are invited to contemplate the fruitfulness of the trees on every side. This, I believe, speaks to the Church herself being fruitful through the many that are born of baptism through the womb of the Church. This fruitfulness can only be possible if the Church is missionary, bringing all people to know the loving mercy of our Lord Jesus Christ. This missionary dimension of the Church is integral to priesthood, as it is integral to the whole people of God. There is another level to the fruit that is integral to our Chrism Mass. The fruit of the tree is necessary to produce the oil that we will bless and consecrate today. Through the Oil of Catechumens, the Church welcomes Adam's children who were estranged from God, marking them to be seekers of God and His Kingdom. Those preparing to be baptised are strengthened through this anointing, to turn away from evil, temptation and sin. They are set on the path to Christ.

Through the Oil of the Sick that we will bless today, the infirmed will be healed, their sins will be forgiven and they will be reconciled with God. This is the fruitfulness of the tree and its role in the healing of the nations. Through the Oil of Sacred Chrism that we will consecrate today, the baptised will be sent on mission as Prophet, Priest and King. The confirmed will be sealed and receive the Holy Spirit in its seven-fold grace and priests will be brought forth to praise the glory of God. The fruit of the tree, indeed, brings healing to the nations. It is medicinal for body and soul. It is what we priests use to make the Church fruitful.

We live in a strange, strange time. There were eras in the Church that considered themselves strange eras, but we are living in an electronic era where we know what is happening elsewhere and information flows fast. So we know the extent of the challenge that we are facing with COVID. We also know the impact it has had upon the Church and the impact it has had upon the priests. We know the isolation that many felt in that time of lockdown and the angst that we carried for our people, as our people struggled with being locked down, as children struggled with education because they did not have devices, and therefore, could not participate in the education process. We know the pain that we have carried in these nine to ten months of COVID and the challenge that it has been as we have innovated and tried new things; things that have never been tried before and things that have never been seen before. But as we see the challenge that we are facing in this time of COVID, I pray and I beg that we also see this as an incredible moment, a time and an opportunity of grace.

People who were unready to hear the gospel before because of the busyness of their lives and the security in which they lived, are now open to hearing the Gospel of Jesus Christ in a new way. And these people need a preacher. A preacher who would take the Old and the New Testaments and bring it to them in a way that it would be medicinal for their souls and revive that which was dead. These people need a preacher who would allow the Testaments which have been handed down, to come alive in such a way that their lives would come to life again with Christ.

This typology of Ezekiel, of the beautiful stream that comes from Jesus, from the water flowing from His side also speaks of the seven great mysteries that Christ entrusted to His Church; that is how the water flows – through these seven great mysteries. And we, as priests, are the custodians of the mystery, custodians of these seven flowing streams of grace, the Seven Sacraments that have been entrusted to us, that we are to administer to the people of God. And it is through these sacraments – through these seven streams, these seven ways of encountering God – that we have been asked as priests to allow the water to flow and to flow deeply into the lives of our people, that they may drink and drink deeply from the well-spring of salvation and come to know the love and the grace of Our Lord Jesus Christ. To see the sacrament as an encounter with God is to be excited in every moment and at every opportunity that we have or create to bring people to encounter Christ through these sacraments; that is the role of the priest. It is why we were ordained and our hands consecrated, so that we can be used by Him to allow this water, which started to flow in Jerusalem, to flow to every village, to every nook and cranny in this wonderful twin-island republic of Trinidad and Tobago. Everywhere we go in this land this water must flow, this grace must happen, our people must come to wade in its water, to eat of the fruit, to use the leaves that are medicinal and come to life in Christ again. Brothers, this is not the moment to hold back! This is not the moment to retreat! This is not the moment to become reticent about our role as priests in this land. This is the moment where we must boldly live out what has been given and entrusted into our hands because people are hungry, they are thirsty, they are starving for the word of God and for the word of life and for the food of their stomachs. People are hungry! They need us!

As we look and see what has happened in our country over the COVID time, many hungry people had jobs in March and are now plunged into hopelessness. We became a sign of hope for many, many people, but that hopelessness has not ended. Many people who lived securely in March are no longer living securely now. Remember the poor! Remember the poor! In whatever you do, remember the poor! Remember that theirs is the face and the image of Jesus Christ. And remember that, in their faces, we have the privilege of contemplating Christ and seeing Christ with our own eyes. As we remember the poor and we remember this beautiful stream and the seven great mysteries – the grace of the sacramental system, the great mysteries entrusted to our hands – we must also remember that the beautiful stream is a symbol of the Holy Spirit. And we must remember that we can do nothing without God's Holy Spirit: "Take back Your Spirit, O Lord, and we shall return to the dust from which we came".

So, before we come to the renewal of our vows, before we come to say again that we are ready, willing and able to live as priests, before we come to that moment where we commit ourselves again, not to shrink back, but to go forward into the world bringing God's incredible love, let us pray for God's Holy Spirit to come afresh upon us. Let us pray for an outpouring of the Holy Spirit upon us as a Presbyterate and us as a Church here in Trinidad and Tobago. That the same Holy Spirit, who birthed the Church at Pentecost and sent her out into mission, will birth inside of us a desire and a fire for spreading God's incredible love to all people in this wonderful twin-island republic in which we live. Let us pray that God's Holy Spirit, the Spirit of sanctification, may make us holy priests. Let us also pray that this Holy Spirit, giving gifts for mission, will give us every gift that we need in these days to allow the incredible love of our God to be known by all His people.

We open wide our hearts today and pray, beg, beseech God: "Send forth Your Spirit upon us, O Lord! Send forth Your Spirit upon us, O Lord", that we can become the priests that Your Church here in Trinidad and Tobago needs for this time and for this people. Amen.

CONCLUSION

During the ninety days of the lockdown of the Church, many people found solace in the Daily Mass. The notes and comments received were overwhelming. I trust that this book has brought back fond memories, stirred your appetite and allowed you to delve even deeper into the mysteries of faith.

When the lockdown began, I instinctively took to the televised Mass every day. This was both a grace and a burden. A grace because people had no fixed point of reference in their day and the Daily Mass provided this. A stable routine around which the day hinged. This also meant that there was a hunger and an expectation that was unconscious. The receptivity of people brought out the teacher and homilist in me. Because of the unusual circumstances, I began giving longer and more in-depth homilies during the week. This meant doing more and more preparation every day for the homily of the next day.

In each day, God's grace was at work in the preparation and the homily. I was still leading the Church, and thus, doing 10-hour days to keep up with meetings and initiatives that were pressing. At the end of the day, I would then turn to the homily of the next day and begin delving into the Scriptural text and the commentaries.

The routine became a labour of love, an excitement to see what was hidden in the text that would unfold. Each day, new insights emerged and they came forth in the preaching. That was grace for me and for the congregation that tuned in from all over the world.

"Christ Our Victory In the Desert" became the brand. We were plunged into a desert because of COVID, but the Word of God in the desert brought life to so many. As you read these homilies, relive the experience of grace that we all shared in that unique time. I pray that they feed you as richly now as when we were together in the desert during that first Lent. Let us all pray that the Food provided for our Journey may bring renewed life to us and to the whole Church.

REFERENCES

This work was composed as an oral text and, therefore, did not cite references. In an oral work, it is not the custom to cite sources, especially if they are commentaries or works of biblical exploration. A written work has different requirements. I used a wide array of commentaries to drill down into each text and bring forth the homily. All biblical texts are from the Jerusalem Bible. Below are some of the commentaries and works that were used to explore the biblical texts.

Aquinas, Thomas. (1845). *Catena Aurea: Commentary on the Four Gospels, Collected out of the Works of the Fathers: St. John*. (J. H. Newman, Ed.) (Vol. 4,). Oxford: John Henry Parker.

Beasley-Murray, G. R. (1999). *Word Biblical Commentary, Volume 36: St. John*. Dallas: Word, Incorporated.

Baltzer, K. (2001). *Deutero-Isaiah: a commentary on Isaiah 40–55*. (P. Machinist, Ed.). Minneapolis, MN: Fortress Press.

Bovon, F. (2012). *Luke 3: A Commentary on the Gospel of Luke 19:28–24:53*. (H. Koester, Ed., J. Crouch, Trans.). Minneapolis, MN: Fortress Press.

Chrysostom, John. (1957). *Commentary on Saint John the Apostle and Evangelist: Homilies 1–47*. (T. A. Goggin, Trans.) (Vol. 33, p. 423). Washington, DC: The Catholic University of America Press.

Collins, A. Y., & Attridge, H. W. (2007). *Mark: A Commentary on the Gospel of Mark*. Minneapolis, MN: Fortress Press.

Fee, G. D., & Hubbard, R. L., Jr. (Eds.). (2011). *The Eerdmans Companion to the Bible*. Grand Rapids, MI; Cambridge, U.K.: William B. Eerdmans Publishing Company.

Gadenz, P. T. (2018). *The Gospel of Luke*. (P. S. Williamson & M. Healy, Eds.). Grand Rapids, MI: Baker Academic: A Division of Baker Publishing Group.

Haenchen, Ernst, (1984). *John 1: A Commentary on the Gospel of John, Chapters 1-6*. Philadelphia: Fortress Press.

Haenchen, E., Funk, R. W., & Busse, U. (1984). *John 2: A Commentary on the Gospel of John Chapters 7-21*. Philadelphia: Fortress Press.

Holladay, W. L. (1986). *Jeremiah 1: a commentary on the Book of the Prophet Jeremiah, chapters 1–25*. (P. D. Hanson, Ed.) Philadelphia: Fortress Press.

Holladay, W. L. (1989). *Jeremiah 2: a commentary on the Book of the Prophet Jeremiah, chapters 26–52*. (P. D. Hanson, Ed.) Minneapolis, MN: Fortress Press.

Jamieson, R., Fausset, A. R., & Brown, D. (1997). *Commentary Critical and Explanatory on the Whole Bible* (Vol. 2). Oak Harbor, WA: Logos Research Systems, Inc.

Keil, C. F., & Delitzsch, F. (1996). *Commentary on the Old Testament* (Vol. 7, p). Peabody, MA: Hendrickson.

Lenski, R. C. H. (1961). *The Interpretation of St. John's Gospel*. Minneapolis, MN: Augsburg Publishing House.

Leonard, W. (1953). "The Gospel of Jesus Christ according to St John." In B. Orchard & E. F. Sutcliffe (Eds.), *A Catholic Commentary on Holy Scripture* (p. 991). Toronto; New York; Edinburgh: Thomas Nelson.

Luz, U. (2005). *Matthew 21–28: A Commentary*. (H. Koester, Ed.) Minneapolis, MN: Augsburg.

Luz, U. (2001). *Matthew 8-20: A Commentary*. (H. Koester, Ed.). Minneapolis, MN: Augsburg.

Paul, S. M. (2012). *Isaiah 40–66: Translation and Commentary*. Grand Rapids, MI; Cambridge, UK: William B. Eerdmans Publishing Company.

Pitre, Brant. *The Eucharist in the Gospel of John*. Catholic Productions. [MP3]

Pitre, Brant. *The Jewish Roots of Holy Week: The 7 Last Days of Jesus*. Catholic Productions. [MP3]

Pitre, Brant. *The Jewish Roots of Jesus' Death and Resurrection*. Catholic Productions. [MP3]

Pitre, Brant. *Jesus and the Jewish Roots of the Eucharist*, Image, First Edition, 2011.

Ratzinger, J. (2011). *Jesus of Nazareth: Part Two: Holy Week: From the Entrance into Jerusalem to the Resurrection* (p. xiii). San Francisco: Ignatius Press.

Roberts, A., Donaldson, J., & Coxe, A. C. (Eds.). (1886). *Fathers of the Third Century: Hippolytus, Cyprian, Novatian, Appendix* (Vol. 5,). Buffalo, NY: Christian Literature Company.

Schaff, Phillip; John Chrysostom. *Nicene and Post-Nicene Fathers 1.14 Saint Chrysostom: Homilies on the Gospel of St. John and Epistle to the Hebrews*. Christian Literature Company.

Schaff, P. (Ed.), Gibb, J. & Innes, J. (Trans.), *St. Augustine: Homilies on the Gospel of John, Homilies on the First Epistle of John, Soliloquies* (Vol. 7, p. 158). New York: Christian Literature Company.

O'Flynn, J. A. (1953). "The Gospel of Jesus Christ According to St Mark." In B. Orchard & E. F. Sutcliffe (Eds.), *A Catholic Commentary on Holy Scripture* (p. 930). Toronto; New York; Edinburgh: Thomas Nelson.

Verbum Catholic Bible Study, Catholic library

Winer, Lisa (Ed), 2009. *Dictionary of the English/Creole of Trinidad and Tobago*. Montreal: McGill-Queen's University Press.

Zimmerli, W. (1979–). *Ezekiel: A Commentary on the Book of the Prophet Ezekiel*. (F. M. Cross & K. Baltzer, Eds.) Philadelphia: Fortress Press.

Made in the USA
Middletown, DE
30 November 2022

15868895R00109